SCHOLASTIC

YEAR IN SPORTS

2019

Copyright © 2018 by Shoreline Publishing Group LLC

ISBN 978-1-338-30979-9

10 9 8 7 6 5 4 3 2 1   18 19 20 21 22

Printed in the U.S.A.   40
First edition, December 2018

Produced by Shoreline Publishing Group LLC

Due to the publication date, records, results, and statistics are current as of early August 2018.

Contents

Gold and a Cup

Are you still tired? We are! Now *THAT* was a Year in Sports! You couldn't go near a TV, a screen, your phone, or even, you know, look at one of those newspaper things your parents talk about . . . without seeing another amazing sports moment!

The year started out with a thrilling Super Bowl. Who knew quarterbacks could also catch touchdown passes? Then an ageless superstar won his 20th Grand Slam tennis final! Before you could catch your breath, the Winter Olympics roared in! For two-plus weeks, fans around the world thrilled to the high-flying feats of snowboarders, skiers, and skaters. The hockey tournaments created nightly highlights. And the world saw an example it could follow as North and South Koreans marched together in peace.

Back in the United States, the NCAA basketball tournaments were packed with excitement. Did you see when a No. 16 seed upset a No. 1 . . . for the first time ever? Did you check out the amazing comebacks and surprising stars? And what about that last-second shot to win the women's tournament? Well, as with the Olympics, if you missed all that, we've got it in here.

The NBA season rolled into the playoffs with everyone's eye on the defending champs. Sometimes in sports repeating can be even harder than winning for the first time. The Golden State Warriors, however, had no problem bringing back another trophy.

Alina Zagitova leaped to Olympic gold.

France's Kylian Mbappé thrilled French fans with a goal in the World Cup final.

In the NHL, the story was in Las Vegas. The new team there shocked everyone by being, well . . . great! No first-year team had ever done as well as the Golden Knights. In the Stanley Cup Final, though, it was the Washington Capitals that carried home the championship. Good run by the Knights, though!

Even as hoopsters and hockey heroes were battling, the world turned its eyes to the biggest event of the year—the 2018 World Cup! More than a billion people spent time watching some of the soccer games. Many of them said it was the best World Cup ever. Of course, the folks in France *definitely* said that!

And that's not even to mention great golf, amazing action sports, a world rugby championship, a Triple Crown horse, thrilling motor sports racing, and much more. (And we didn't even mention the 2017 World Series, which really began our Year in Sports with some of the most memorable games in recent years.)

We just got tired writing all that . . . imagine re-living it! Wait . . . you don't have to imagine it, you just have to turn the page and start reading. Meanwhile, we're watching our screens to enjoy another YEAR IN SPORTS!

TOP 10 MOMENTS IN SPORTS

Sure, we wish we could make that Top 100! But we only have room for ten, so that's what we'll start with. These all happened from September 2017 through August 2018. Did your favorite moment make the list? Keep watching sports for more top moments as the new sports year gets going!

10 MARVELOUS MARTIN *Martin Truex, Jr., was "the man" for most of the 2017 NASCAR season. He had eight wins in all and finished in the top five in 19 of 38 races. His biggest win came in the season's final race, the Chase for the Cup championship in Miami. The veteran won his first NASCAR championship by roaring to the checkered flag before doing celebration donuts!*

9 **SNOW GOOD!** *There were a lot of great stories from the 2018 Winter Olympics (see more on page 10 and starting on page 48), but two snowboard stars stood out to make our Top Ten list.* **Chloe Kim** *(right) as one of the youngest competitors, but she soared the highest. The 17-year-old won the women's half-pipe with a mix of amazing spins and great landings.* **Shaun White** *(above) first won world attention as a teenager, but now he's an "old" veteran at 31. He became the first person to win three snowboard golds with a stunning final run in the half-pipe.*

8 **BUZZER-BEATER!** *The clock was ticking down in the women's NCAA basketball final. Notre Dame had the ball in the hands of its star,* **Akire Ogunbowale**. *Just two days before, she had hit a buzzer-beater to send her team to the championship game. Could she do it again? Yes! In one of the most dramatic finishes ever, her three-point shot went in with 0.0 seconds left. Notre Dame beat Mississippi State 61–58.*

7

GOOD MOVE, COACH! *What do you do if your team is struggling in the national championship game? Alabama coach Nick Saban asked himself that question. His answer was surprising . . . and a winner. He sent in a freshman quarterback, Tua Tagovailoa (right), after halftime. The young lefthander responded with great success. He led the Crimson Tide to a game-tying TD. In overtime, he launched a 41-yard pass that won the school's fifth national title in nine seasons.*

6 **HOCKEY HEROES** *The US women's hockey team had been disappointed over and over in the Olympics. After winning the gold in 1998, the team had been knocked out of the top spot by Canada several times. In 2018, the US got another chance to beat their rival. A third-period goal tied the game at 2–2. Twenty extra minutes did not decide the winner. It came down to a shootout.* **Jocelyne Lamoureux-Davidson** *made the shot shown here. Then US goalie* **Maddie Rooney** *stopped the final Canadian shooter to clinch the gold medal for the Americans.*

5 REIGN IN THE RAIN

Horse racing fans had waited a long time for Triple Crown winner **American Pharoah***; that horse broke a 37-year streak of no Triple Crowns. But just three years later, those fans got another.* **Justify** *galloped to victory in the 2018 Belmont Stakes to capture the elusive racing prize. Trainer* **Bob Baffert** *became the second person to guide a pair of Triple Crown winners.*

4

EAGLES FLY! *The Patriots were in the Super Bowl . . . again. So that means Tom Brady & Co. took home the trophy, right? Not so fast. The high-flying Philadelphia Eagles, led by the surprising QB Nick Foles, knocked off the favored Pats 41–33 in Super Bowl LII. Foles was named the game's MVP after throwing three TD passes . . . and even catching one himself! The trick play was a key turning point as the Eagles won the team's first Super Bowl title.*

3

TWO GREAT GAMES *The 2017 World Series featured two of the most entertaining games in recent baseball history. Game 7, which won it all for the Houston Astros, was, oddly, one of the least interesting of a great series. In Game 2, the Los Angeles Dodgers thought they had it in the bag. Houston rallied, though, and won in 11 thrilling innings. The teams combined for seven runs in the two extra innings before Houston won 7–6. Game 5 was even wilder. The game was tied at 4–4, 7–7, 8–8, and 12–12 before Houston's run in the bottom of the 10th was the difference in a 13–12 final.*

had been 135 games played between the No. 16 and No. 1 seeds. The top seed had won ALL of those games. 135–0. Then came the **Retrievers**. The University of Maryland—Baltimore County had never even been in the tournament. Its opponent, Virginia, had been in 21. No one gave UMBC any chance. But they didn't care. The small school shocked Virginia and became the first No. 16 seed to defeat a No. 1 seed. It really was March Madness!

1

VIVE LA FRANCE! *The biggest sporting event in the world wrapped up on July 15 in Moscow. The World Cup included the top 32 national teams and was watched by more than 1 billion people over the course of a month of games. The final match was favored France against underdog Croatia. France poured in four goals and dominated play. Croatia scored once in each half, but it was not enough. For the second time ever, France held up the World Cup trophy as champions!*

F F F

NFL

THE EAGLES HAVE LANDED!
Philadelphia tight end Zach Ertz dove into the end zone late in Super Bowl LII. His touchdown gave Philly the go-ahead points. Then they held off the New England Patriots and claimed their first-ever Super Bowl title. It was also the team's first NFL championship since 1960!

2017: A Philly Special

Every NFL season is like week after week of birthday parties. With every weekend's games, it's like opening another set of new and unexpected presents. The 2017 season was no exception, as surprise after surprise popped up.

For example, only four teams that made the playoffs in 2016 made the postseason in 2017. Among the other 2016 playoff teams, the Giants, Cowboys, and Dolphins all took nosedives in 2017 and had to watch the postseason at home.

Meanwhile, some other teams turned their fortunes around. Out West, the biggest story was the rise of the Los Angeles Rams. They won only four games in 2016, and then-rookie QB **Jared Goff** often looked lost. In the offseason, the team brought in **Sean McVay** as the youngest coach in modern NFL history and he worked his magic. The Rams thrilled their fans by winning 11 games and making the playoffs for the first time since 2004.

Down South, the Jacksonville Jaguars were crafting their own return to glory. Nicknamed "Sacks-onville" for their hard-hitting defense, the Jags went from three wins in 2016 to 10 in 2017 and made it all the way to the AFC Championship Game.

In the East, the Buffalo Bills had gone almost 20 years since their last playoff game. On the final Sunday of the season, the

Tyrod Taylor led the Bills to a surprise playoff spot.

Jared Goff impressed in LA.

Bengals upset Baltimore. That gave the Bills the final playoff spot. Grateful Buffalo fans donated thousands of dollars to Bengals QB **Andy Dalton's** charity!

The Eagles were another rising team, thanks to second-year star QB **Carson Wentz**. But he was lost to a knee injury in December, leaving the team in the hands of backup **Nick Foles**. Turn a few pages to see how that turned out!

Back on the field, everyone expected the great **Tom Brady**, who won his third NFL MVP award, to carry the Patriots to another Super Bowl trophy. A certain green-and-white team, though, had other ideas.

196

The number of regular-season wins by Patriots QB **Tom Brady** — a new NFL record. Among his other stats, Brady won 58 games in December, the most by a QB in any single month!

2017 Final Regular-Season Standings

AFC EAST			AFC NORTH			AFC SOUTH			AFC WEST		
Patriots	13–3		Steelers	13–3		Jaguars	10–6		Chiefs	10–6	
Bills	9–7		Ravens	9–7		Titans	9–7		Chargers	9–7	
Dolphins	6–10		Bengals	7–9		Colts	4–12		Raiders	6–10	
Jets	5–11		Browns	0–16		Texans	4–12		Broncos	5–11	

NFC EAST			NFC NORTH			NFC SOUTH			NFC WEST		
Eagles	13–3		Vikings	13–3		Saints	11–5		Rams	11–5	
Cowboys	9–7		Lions	9–7		Panthers	11–5		Seahawks	9–7	
Redskins	7–9		Packers	7–9		Falcons	10–6		Cardinals	8–8	
Giants	3–13		Bears	5–11		Buccaneers	5–11		49ers	6–10	

2017 Playoffs

Wild Card Weekend

Titans 22, Chiefs 21

The Titans trailed 21–3 at halftime on the road. QB **Marcus Mariota** led a second-half comeback that included one of the wildest plays of the year. Near the goal line, he threw a pass that was tipped. Mariota snagged it before it hit the ground and dove in for a score. He caught his own TD pass!

Falcons 26, Rams 13

LA's surprise season ended suddenly. The defending NFC-champion Falcons used their experience–and four **Matt Bryant** field goals–to beat the Rams.

Jaguars 10, Bills 3

Offense took this game off, and the Jags' defense proved to be more than enough to win. It was Buffalo's first playoff game in 18 seasons, so maybe they were a little rusty!

Saints 31, Panthers 26

A great game by veteran QB **Drew Brees** gave the Saints a victory. Brees threw for 376 yards and 2 TDs, while the Saints' D sacked QB **Cam Newton** four times.

Divisional Playoffs

Vikings 29, Saints 24

This one ended with the play of the season. The Vikings trailed 24–23 with just a few seconds left when QB **Case Keenum** heaved a long pass toward the sideline. **Stefon Diggs** leaped and caught it. After he came down, he realized there was no one between him and the goal line. The Saints defenders had dived at

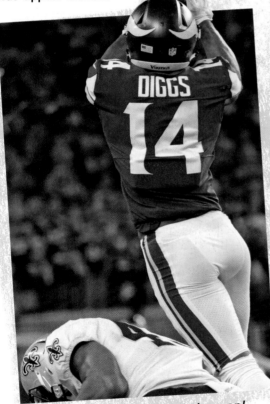

Diggs made a miracle happen!

him and missed! Diggs scampered home with a shocking 61-yard TD pass quickly nicknamed the Minnesota Miracle!

Eagles 15, Falcons 10

Philadelphia shut down Atlanta's powerful offense. The Eagles got three field goals from rookie **Jake Elliott**. In the final minute, Atlanta's **Julio Jones** missed a possible game-winning catch.

Jaguars 45, Steelers 42

Jacksonville dominated the Steelers, thanks to 3 TD runs by rookie **Leonard Fournette** and some big plays on defense. Pittsburgh QB **Ben Roethlisberger** tried to rally his team, but his 5 TD passes were not enough.

Patriots 35, Titans 14

Tom Brady showed why he has won five Super Bowls. He carved up Tennessee's defense for 337 yards and 3 TD passes. Brady set an NFL record with his 10th career 3-TD playoff game.

Conference Championships

Patriots 24, Jaguars 20

Once again, Brady was just too much. The four-time Super Bowl MVP set up another shot at a trophy. He hit **Danny Amendola** with a four-yard pass for the game-winning score. That sent **Brady** to his record eighth Super Bowl.

Amendola's grab clinched the AFC title.

Eagles 38, Vikings 7

The Minnesota Miracle was over. Led by a great game from QB **Nick Foles**, Philadelphia crushed the Vikings. Foles shredded the Vikings' top-rated defense for 3 TDs and 357 yards passing. He got help from WR **Alshon Jeffrey**, who made great leaping grabs for two of those scores. Tight end **Zach Ertz** had 93 yards receiving, too. Philly's D picked off **Keenum** twice and recovered a fumble. The Eagles headed to their first Super Bowl in 13 seasons.

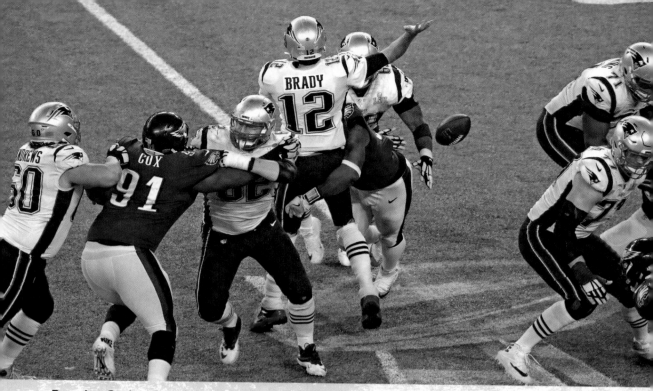

Brandon Graham's strip of Brady was a key play.

Super Bowl LII

Until this game, if you scored 33 points in a Super Bowl, you won. Not this time.

Until this game, if you gained more than 600 yards on offense, you won. Not just in the playoffs . . . in ANY NFL game. Just not this time.

Until this game, the Philadelphia Eagles had not won an NFL title since 1960.

All those things changed thanks to the Eagles' unstoppable offense. Philly outscored the powerful Patriots 41–33. The game featured tons of amazing plays but only one punt. It was a record-setting offensive show. The two teams combined for 1,151 total yards. That was not just a playoff record . . . it was an all-time record for *any* NFL game! Yet in a game that featured

such fireworks, it was a defensive play that proved to be the biggest one of all.

The Eagles were up 15–12 late in the second quarter when they made their first huge play. On fourth-and-goal, they went for it instead of taking an easy field goal. After a timeout, they shocked the Patriots and all the fans with a trick play. QB **Nick Foles** moved to the end of the offensive line. The snap went directly to RB **Corey Clement**. As he ran left, he pitched the ball to TE **Trey Burton**, who threw it to Foles! He had slipped unnoticed into the end zone and made his first-ever TD catch. Coach **Doug Pederson** said after the game that the play was called "Philly Special"!

613

That is the new Super Bowl record for total yards on offense by a team, set by the Patriots in this game. It's also the most yards ever in a Super Bowl by a losing team (of course!). **Tom Brady** set a single-game Super Bowl record with 505 passing yards, too.

The scoring continued in the second half with Philly answering every time **Tom Brady** and the Patriots charged back. After only one catch in the first half, New England TE **Rob Gronkowski** had a huge second half. He snagged eight passes, including two for scores. Philly countered with a touchdown catch by Clement and **Jake Elliott**'s second field goal.

The Patriots took their first lead of the game on Gronk's second TD. Foles then led the Eagles on a long drive that included a clutch play to convert a fourth-and-one situation. With 2:21 left in the game, from the 11-yard line, he hit TE **Zach Ertz**, who dove into the end zone to put the Eagles back on top.

Then came the big defensive play. Brady, the comeback king, was on the move to retake the lead. **Brandon Graham** swept around from behind and reached out to knock the ball from Brady's hands. Philly recovered and a few plays later Elliott added the clinching field goal. On the game's final play, a Hail Mary from Brady to Gronk fell incomplete.

The Eagles were champs!

What a Story!

In the 52-year history of the Super Bowl, only one other QB has started in fewer regular-season games before taking the field for the big game. **Nick Foles** (right) had to take over after starter **Carson Wentz** went down in Week 14. Foles was only so-so in his first few games in charge in Philly. In the playoffs, though, he was lights-out. In the Super Bowl, he threw for 373 yards and 3 TDs. He was picked off once, but that came on a ball tipped by his own receiver to the Patriots! The surprise star was calm and cool and came through. He was an easy choice as Super Bowl MVP.

2017 Stats Leaders

1,327 RUSHING YARDS
Kareem Hunt, Chiefs

13 RUSHING TDS
Todd Gurley, Rams

1,533 RECEIVING YARDS
Antonio Brown, Steelers

112 RECEPTIONS
Jarvis Landry, Dolphins

13 RECEIVING TDS
DeAndre Hopkins, Texans

4,577 PASSING YARDS
Tom Brady, Patriots

34 TD PASSES
Russell Wilson, Seahawks

39 FIELD GOALS
Robbie Gould, 49ers

158 POINTS
Greg Zuerlein, Rams

144 TACKLES
Preston Brown, Bills

17.0 SACKS
Chandler Jones, Cardinals

8 INTERCEPTIONS
Kevin Byard, Titans
Darius Slay, Lions

Antonio Brown

Award Winners

MVP
TOM BRADY, QB
PATRIOTS

OFFENSIVE PLAYER OF THE YEAR
TODD GURLEY, RB
RAMS

DEFENSIVE PLAYER OF THE YEAR
AARON DONALD, DT
RAMS

OFFENSIVE ROOKIE OF THE YEAR
ALVIN KAMARA, RB
SAINTS

DEFENSIVE ROOKIE OF THE YEAR
MARSHON LATTIMORE, CB
SAINTS

COMEBACK PLAYER OF THE YEAR
KEENAN ALLEN
CHARGERS

COACH OF THE YEAR
SEAN McVAY
RAMS

Aaron Donald

CLUTCH PERFORMER OF THE YEAR
DREW BREES, QB
SAINTS

WALTER PAYTON NFL MAN OF THE YEAR (COMMUNITY SERVICE)
J. J. WATT, DE
TEXANS

1st Quarter

WEEKS 1-4

★ Kid Coach Wins Big: At 31, new LA Rams coach **Sean McVay** became the youngest in NFL history. He showed that he knows what he's doing in Week 1, leading the Rams to a 46–9 defeat of the Indianapolis Colts. The Rams' D scored two touchdowns and a safety, while former No. 1 pick QB **Jared Goff** got his first win as a starter.

★ Dancin' Raider: RB **Marshawn Lynch** was known as "Beast Mode" when he was with Seattle. After a year off, he came back to play with the Raiders. In their second game, a 45–20 win over the Jets, he scored his first Oakland TD. On the sidelines later in the game, he got the crowd on its feet with a hair-waving, foot-stomping, celebration dance. How about "Dance Mode"?

★ Top Tight End: The LA Chargers' **Antonio Gates** caught his 112th career TD pass. He passed **Tony Gonzalez** as the NFL's all-time leader among tight ends. The bad news for the future Hall of Famer was that his team lost to the Dolphins 19–17.

★ Fantastic Finishes: A stack of amazing endings came in games played in Week 3. Philadelphia kicker **Jake Elliott** hit a 61-yard field goal

to lift his team over the Giants 27–24. It was the longest final-play game-winner ever by a rookie. Megastar QB **Tom Brady** (naturally!) led a final drive that ended with a 25-yard TD pass to **Brandin Cooks**. That play helped New England come back to beat Houston 36–33. The Chicago Bears won in overtime when **Jordan Howard** ran in from 19 yards to upset Pittsburgh 23–17. And a 72-yard pass from Green Bay's **Aaron Rodgers** to **Geronimo Allison** led to a game-winning field goal by **Mason Crosby** in overtime over Cincinnati. The Packers won 27–24.

★ In the Hunt: Kansas City rookie running back **Kareem Hunt** scored on a 69-yard run in the Chiefs' 24–10 win over the Chargers. He became the first player ever with scores of 50 or more yards in each of his first three NFL games.

★ Ram Tough: In 2015 and 2016 combined, the LA Rams scored 30 or more points in a game three times. With a shocking 35–30 win on the road over Dallas, the Rams had three such games in 2017 alone! Goff continued to improve, RB **Todd Gurley** had 215 yards from scrimmage, and **Greg Zeurlein** tied a team record with 7 field goals.

Kareem Hunt

2nd Quarter
WEEKS 5-8

✱ Tough Breaks: Three teams lost superstar players to injury. WR **Odell Beckham, Jr.,** broke a leg bone as the Giants fell to 0–5 with a loss to the Chargers. DE **J.J. Watt** also broke a bone in his leg as Houston lost to Kansas City. A week later, Green Bay's playoffs hopes took a big hit in a 23–10 loss to Minnesota. Star QB **Aaron Rodgers** suffered a broken collarbone and was lost for two months.

✱ Not This Again: That's what Atlanta was feeling after losing 20–17 to Miami. As they had done in the Super Bowl, the Falcons were well ahead, 17–0, only to see their opponent roar back for the unexpected win.

✱ Unlucky Niners: San Francisco lost to Washington 26–24. That made it five straight defeats for the 49ers . . . by a total of 13 points! They became the first NFL team ever to drop five in a row by three points or fewer.

✱ Two Times Six: Chicago safety **Eddie Jackson** became the first player ever with two defensive touchdowns of 75 yards or more in the same game. He returned a fumble 75 yards and an interception 76 yards as the Bears beat the Panthers 17–3.

✱ Sacks-onville!: The Jaguars celebrated their defense's new nickname with a 27–0 shutout of Indianapolis. With 10 sacks, the Jags became only the second team in 33 years with two double-digit sack totals in one season! It was also their first shutout since 2006.

✱ Comeback City: Houston and Seattle played one of the best games of the season. They combined for 28 points in the fourth quarter, with both teams coming from behind twice. In the end, Seattle won 41–38 by scoring last, on a pass from **Russell Wilson** to tight end **Jimmy Graham** with 21 seconds left. Houston rookie sensation **Deshaun Watson** had 4 TD tosses. That gave him 19 for the season, the most ever for a player's first seven games. Sadly, Watson hurt his knee in practice the following week and was out for the rest of the season.

Watson set a rookie TD pass record.

3rd Quarter
WEEKS 9–12

Rivers gobbled up Dallas.

✶ Super Saints: New Orleans won its seventh straight game after an 0–2 start by beating Buffalo 47–10. RB **Mark Ingram** ran for 131 yards and 3 touchdowns. The Saints' offense was so good that the team never had to punt!

✶ More Records for Brady: QB **Tom Brady** led New England to a 41–16 defeat of Denver. It was the team's twelfth straight win on the road, tying an AFC record (set by another Patriots team, of course). It was also Brady's 86th win on the road, a new all-time NFL best.

✶ Big Kicks: A pair of kickers made the longest field goals of their careers to win big games for their teams. Pittsburgh's **Chris Boswell** blasted a 53-yarder on the game's final play as the Steelers beat the Packers 31–28. **Phil Dawson**'s game-winner for Arizona went 57 yards. The Cardinals beat the Jaguars 27–24.

✶ Eagles Keep Flying: In Denver's Mile High Stadium, the Eagles flew the highest. They rolled over the Broncos' top-ranked defense 51–23. **Carson Wentz** had his second 4-TD game of the season. **Corey Clement** scored three times for Philadelphia.

✶ Sack City: Atlanta DE **Adrian Clayborn** had 6 sacks, one shy of an NFL record, and also forced 2 fumbles. The Falcons rode his mighty defense to a 27–7 win over Dallas. Atlanta QB **Matt Ryan** reached 40,000 career passing yards in fewer games than anyone in NFL history.

✶ Streak Stopper: The Rams continued to be the NFL's surprise team. They stopped the Saints' eight-game win streak and moved into a tie atop the NFC West with a 26–20 victory. LA used a tough defense to slow down the Saints' powerful offense. QB **Jared Goff** threw for 354 yards and 2 touchdowns.

✶ The Chargers—NOT a Turkey: The Los Angeles Chargers played their first-ever game on Thanksgiving Day and made the most of it. They knocked the stuffing out of the Cowboys 28–6. Chargers QB **Philip Rivers** threw for 434 yards and 3 TDs.

4th Quarter
WEEKS 13-17

★ The Eagles Have Landed: Seattle ended Philadelphia's nine-game winning streak with a 24-10 win. Seahawks QB **Russell Wilson** threw 3 TD passes.

★ Fallen Eagle: Philadelphia won the game, but lost a quarterback. **Carson Wentz** suffered a knee injury as his team beat the Rams 43-35 and was lost for the season. It was a big victory for Philly over a top NFC rival, but the loss of Wentz left fans sad.

★ Panthers Pounce: Carolina won another big NFC showdown, beating Minnesota 31-24. Panthers QB **Cam Newton** had a 62-yard run late in the game that set up **Jonathan Stewart**'s third rushing TD. A Saints loss earlier put the Panthers in a tie for the top spot in the NFC South.

★ Playoffs, Here We Come: The surprising Jaguars stomped on divison-rival Houston 45-7. That gave Jacksonville its first playoff spot since 2007!

★ Four in a Row: QB **Jimmy Garoppolo** was the NFL's surprise star late in the season. The former Patriots' backup led the 49ers to five straight wins after taking over as the starter. The second-to-last of those was an upset of the Jaguars, who were headed for the playoffs. "Jimmy G" helped the Niners put up a season-high 44 points against the Jags' highly rated defense.

★ Thank You, Bengals!: That's what Buffalo fans were saying after Cincinnati's shocking Week 17 win over Baltimore. On a fourth-and-12 with less than a minute left, the Bengals scored a 49-yard, game-winning TD! The sudden 31-27 loss left the Ravens out of the playoffs and let the Bills back in for the first time since 1999!

★ A Titan-ic Win: Tennessee returned to the playoffs with a big 15-10 win over Jacksonville. The Titans have not reached the postseason since 2008. Four turnovers forced by the Titans' D were key to the victory.

★ Ouch: Cleveland tied a record no team wants to have. The Browns became the second team ever to finish 0-16 by losing to the Steelers 28-24. They matched the 2008 Lions in this saddest of categories.

Cam Newton

2017: New Records

Every season, the NFL racks up more numbers than a calculator factory. Here are some of the most memorable new records or achievements in 2017.

PATRIOTS POWER: With 13 wins, the Patriots became the first team in NFL history with 12 or more wins in eight straight seasons.

MR. 100: Antonio Brown of Pittsburgh became the only player in NFL history with five consecutive 100-catch seasons.

ON TARGET: Saints QB **Drew Brees** completed 72.0 percent of his attempts. That's the best single-season rate ever.

GOOD STREAK: Keenan Allen of the Chargers was the first player ever to have 10 catches, 100 receiving yards, and a TD catch for three games in a row.

LONG EAGLE: Philly kicker **Jake Elliott**'s 61-yard field goal in Week 3 was the longest ever by a rookie.

TERRIFIC TWOSOME: Saints RBs **Alvin Kamara** and **Mark Ingram** each topped 1,500 yards from scrimmage. That was the first time in league history that RB teammates did so.

Drew
Brees

FANTASY STARS

Fans around the country watched their favorite NFL teams . . . and their own fantasy teams. Here were the top-scoring fantasy players, according to NFL.com.

POS.	PLAYER	POINTS
QB	Russell Wilson	347.9
RB	Todd Gurley	319.3
WR	DeAndre Hopkins	213.8
TE	Rob Gronkowski	158.4
K	Greg Zuerlein	170.0
DEF	Jaguars	203.0

2018 Hall of Fame

Football fans welcomed this class of stars to the Pro Football Hall of Fame.

Bobby Beathard As a general manager, he led three franchises (Dolphins, Redskins, Chargers) to the Super Bowl. Those teams combined to win four championships.

LB Robert Brazile One of the best all-around linebackers of the 1970s, Brazile led the Houston Oilers (now the Tennessee Titans) to some of their most successful seasons.

S Brian Dawkins This multi-talented defensive back played in nine Pro Bowls and helped the Eagles reach five NFC Championship Games.

G Jerry Kramer The Packers won five NFL titles in the 1960s, and this powerful blocker was a key part of all of them. His role in the Packers Sweep helped the team's running game go.

LB Ray Lewis A hard-hitting tackler and inspirational leader, Lewis was named to 13 Pro Bowls and was a rare defensive player to win Super Bowl MVP (XXXV).

WR Randy Moss Tall and fast, Moss was a record-setting star for five teams. His 23 TD catches in 2007 are a single-season record.

WR Terrell Owens "T.O." was one of the most successful receivers of a pass-happy

Randy Moss

era. His 153 career TD catches are third all-time, while his 15,934 receiving yards are second most.

LB Brian Urlacher Chicago has boasted some of the greatest defensive players in NFL history. But this powerful Bear is the team's all-time leading tackler as well as an eight-time Pro Bowl selection.

For the Record

Super Bowl Winners

GAME	SEASON	WINNING TEAM	LOSING TEAM	SCORE	SITE
LII	2017	**Philadelphia**	New England	41–33	Minneapolis
LI	2016	**New England**	Atlanta	34–28(OT)	Houston
L	2015	**Denver**	Carolina	24–10	Santa Clara
XLIX	2014	**New England**	Seattle	28–24	Glendale, AZ
XLVIII	2013	**Seattle**	Denver	43–8	E. Rutherford, NJ
XLVII	2012	**Baltimore**	San Francisco	34–31	New Orleans
XLVI	2011	**NY Giants**	New England	21–17	Indianapolis
XLV	2010	**Green Bay**	Pittsburgh	31–25	Arlington, TX
XLIV	2009	**New Orleans**	Indianapolis	31–17	Miami
XLIII	2008	**Pittsburgh**	Arizona	27–23	Tampa
XLII	2007	**NY Giants**	New England	17–14	Glendale, AZ
XLI	2006	**Indianapolis**	Chicago	29–17	Miami
XL	2005	**Pittsburgh**	Seattle	21–10	Detroit
XXXIX	2004	**New England**	Philadelphia	24–21	Jacksonville
XXXVIII	2003	**New England**	Carolina	32–29	Houston
XXXVII	2002	**Tampa Bay**	Oakland	48–21	San Diego
XXXVI	2001	**New England**	St. Louis	20–17	New Orleans
XXXV	2000	**Baltimore**	NY Giants	34–7	Tampa
XXXIV	1999	**St. Louis**	Tennessee	23–16	Atlanta
XXXIII	1998	**Denver**	Atlanta	34–19	Miami
XXXII	1997	**Denver**	Green Bay	31–24	San Diego
XXXI	1996	**Green Bay**	New England	35–21	New Orleans
XXX	1995	**Dallas**	Pittsburgh	27–17	Tempe
XXIX	1994	**San Francisco**	San Diego	49–26	Miami

GAME	SEASON	WINNING TEAM	LOSING TEAM	SCORE	SITE
XXVIII	1993	**Dallas**	Buffalo	**30–13**	Atlanta
XXVII	1992	**Dallas**	Buffalo	**52–17**	Pasadena
XXVI	1991	**Washington**	Buffalo	**37–24**	Minneapolis
XXV	1990	**NY Giants**	Buffalo	**20–19**	Tampa
XXIV	1989	**San Francisco**	Denver	**55–10**	New Orleans
XXIII	1988	**San Francisco**	Cincinnati	**20–16**	Miami
XXII	1987	**Washington**	Denver	**42–10**	San Diego
XXI	1986	**NY Giants**	Denver	**39–20**	Pasadena
XX	1985	**Chicago**	New England	**46–10**	New Orleans
XIX	1984	**San Francisco**	Miami	**38–16**	Stanford
XVIII	1983	**LA Raiders**	Washington	**38–9**	Tampa
XVII	1982	**Washington**	Miami	**27–17**	Pasadena
XVI	1981	**San Francisco**	Cincinnati	**26–21**	Pontiac, MI
XV	1980	**Oakland**	Philadelphia	**27–10**	New Orleans
XIV	1979	**Pittsburgh**	Los Angeles	**31–19**	Pasadena
XIII	1978	**Pittsburgh**	Dallas	**35–31**	Miami
XII	1977	**Dallas**	Denver	**27–10**	New Orleans
XI	1976	**Oakland**	Minnesota	**32–14**	Pasadena
X	1975	**Pittsburgh**	Dallas	**21–17**	Miami
IX	1974	**Pittsburgh**	Minnesota	**16–6**	New Orleans
VIII	1973	**Miami**	Minnesota	**24–7**	Houston
VII	1972	**Miami**	Washington	**14–7**	Los Angeles
VI	1971	**Dallas**	Miami	**24–3**	New Orleans
V	1970	**Baltimore**	Dallas	**16–13**	Miami
IV	1969	**Kansas City**	Minnesota	**23–7**	New Orleans
III	1968	**NY Jets**	Baltimore	**16–7**	Miami
II	1967	**Green Bay**	Oakland	**33–14**	Miami
I	1966	**Green Bay**	Kansas City	**35–10**	Los Angeles

COLLEGE FOOTBALL

NO. 6 SHOWS WHO'S NO. 1!
The College Football Championship Game ended with a shocking TD. For the first time, the game went to overtime. After Georgia took the lead, Alabama came through again. DeVonta Smith (above) scored on a 41-yard TD to end the game and make 'Bama the champs!

Another Wild Season!

The College Football Playoff has turned the regular season into a giant race to the final four. Teams with their eye on the finals know that any stumble can cost them.

By the end of the regular season, it seemed like seven or eight teams had a chance to claim one of those four spots. As it turned out, the first weekend in December saw three games that worked just like playoffs: the winning teams sailed into three of the final four slots. And then one familiar football face slipped in the side door to fill the remaining spot.

The road to that weekend saw a lot of bumps and sharp turns, however. Upsets knocked Ohio State and Penn State back a bit. Meanwhile, TCU from the Big 12 became an early-season surprise. A busy November saw multiple teams crawling back into contention. Ohio State won the Big Ten. Clemson rebounded from its October loss to capture the ACC title. Georgia shocked many by dominating the SEC.

Meanwhile, the University

TCU was hot early but did not finish in the top four.

of Central Florida ended the season undefeated. However, they didn't play in a "Power 5" conference. Some fans thought that was not fair. Once again, the Playoff plan turned into a puzzle! The committee that chooses the CFP teams added Alabama over Ohio State for the fourth and final Playoff spot. The four-team Playoffs included two incredible games—see page 42!

2017 TOP 10

1. **Alabama**
2. **Georgia**
3. **Oklahoma**
4. **Clemson**
5. **Ohio State**
6. **UCF**
7. **Wisconsin**
8. **Penn State**
9. **TCU**
10. **Auburn**

A Great Wave

The Iowa football team and its fans made news in 2017 for just waving their hands. A new children's hospital was built next to the Iowa stadium. The top floors peer into the stadium and are filled with kids battling cancer and other serious illnesses. Early in the season, the Iowa team stopped playing during a game and waved up to the kids, who watched from their windows. It quickly became a tradition. Fans joined in, as did opponents and officials. For night games, fans waved their lighted phones. The kids knew that the Hawkeyes were behind them, 100 percent!

MAJOR AWARD WINNERS

HEISMAN TROPHY (OUTSTANDING PLAYER)
MAXWELL AWARD (OUTSTANDING PLAYER)
WALTER CAMP AWARD (OUTSTANDING PLAYER)
DAVEY O'BRIEN (TOP QB)
Baker Mayfield/OKLAHOMA

DOAK WALKER AWARD (RUNNING BACK)
Bryce Love/STANFORD

FRED BILETNIKOFF (RECEIVER)
James Washington
OKLAHOMA ST.

JOHN MACKEY (TIGHT END)
Mark Andrews/OKLAHOMA

VINCE LOMBARDI (LINEMAN)
Jonathan Allen/ALABAMA

CHUCK BEDNARIK (DEFENSIVE PLAYER)
JIM THORPE (DEFENSIVE BACK)
Minkah Fitzpatrick/ALABAMA

BRONKO NAGURSKI (DEFENSIVE PLAYER)
Bradley Chubb
NORTH CAROLINA ST.

LOU GROZA (KICKER)
Matt Gay/UTAH

COACH OF THE YEAR
Scott Frost/UCF

August/September
SEASON HIGHLIGHTS

Jackson battled a squirrel for headlines.

→ A Feel-Good Story: Late in their win over Western Michigan, USC sent in a backup center to snap an extra point attempt. He made a perfect snap . . . and his teammates and the crowd at USC went wild! Why so much excitement? Center **Jake Olson** is blind. He worked out with the team while taking classes, but had never played in a game. With help from Western Michigan (they agreed not to knock Olson over), the play was perfect in more ways than one.

→ Boomer Sooner: One of the biggest early-season matchups was between No. 2 Ohio State and No. 5 Oklahoma. Though played at OSU, the game was all OU.

QB **Baker Mayfield** was nearly perfect, throwing 3 TD passes in the 31–16 win. "It was awful," said OSU coach **Urban Meyer**. Sooners fans disagreed!

→ Third and VERY Long: How do you go from second down and goal at the six-yard line . . . to third and 93?! That's what happened to Louisiana Tech against Mississippi State. A fumbled snap led to a crazy play. Players from both teams rushed to recover the ball, but ended up batting and kicking it down the field over and over. Tech's **Cee Jay Powell** finally fell on the ball . . . at the opposite seven-yard line! That was the capper on Tech's 57–21 loss to MSU.

→ Here Come the Horned Frogs: Unranked to start the season, TCU rocketed into the top 10 by late September. Their biggest move came after a 44–31 upset of Oklahoma State, which was ranked No. 6.

→ Squirrel for Six!: Louisville star **Lamar Jackson** set a school record with his 88th career TD pass in a win over Kent State. But the star of the day was a squirrel that ran nearly the length of the field. The fans went wild as the rodent ran into the Louisville end zone and then stopped, panting and taking in the roar of the crowd!

→ Trojan News: Two teams nicknamed the Trojans had different results on the final day of September. The unranked Troy Trojans pulled off a huge upset, knocking off No. 25 Louisiana State. The No. 5 USC Trojans were on the other end of a surprise, losing to Washington State 30–27.

October
SEASON HIGHLIGHTS

➜ **LB = QB:** When you're No. 3 Oklahoma and your unranked opponent has a linebacker playing quarterback . . . you should win. But Oklahoma was upset anyway! Iowa State's LB **Joel Lanning** split time at quarterback with a freshman walk-on, and led the Cyclones to a huge 38–31 win.

➜ **0-0-0-0-0-0-OT:** That's seven Os! Fans at Western Michigan vs. Buffalo probably thought they were at a basketball game. The final score was 71–68. Here's the catch: The teams needed a record-tying *seven* overtimes to find a winner. It was 31–31 at the end of regular time. Then both teams kept scoring until Western Michigan's **Jarvion Franklin** ran in for a TD after Buffalo could only kick a field goal.

➜ **Unlucky Weekend:** Four top 10 teams fell in shocking upsets in two crazy days. Friday the 13th was bad luck for No. 2 Clemson, which lost to unranked Syracuse 27–24. The defending national champion Tigers fell behind early and could never catch up. The same night, 3–3 California forced 7 turnovers and had 9 sacks while rolling over No. 8 Washington State, 37–3. It was only the second win over a Top 10 team by the Golden Bears in 40 years. Upsets continued on Saturday when No. 5 Washington lost to Arizona State 13–7. LSU then knocked off No. 10 Auburn 27–23.

➜ **Buckeye Comeback:** No. 6 Ohio State trailed No. 2 Penn State 7–0 after the opening kickoff and 14–0 a few minutes later. They were behind all day, including being 11 points down with just under six minutes left. However, OSU QB **J. T. Barrett** was perfect in the fourth quarter, leading three TD drives. The team's last score, a catch by **Marcus Baugh** from Barrett, put them on top for the first time and they held on for the unlikely win.

➜ **Bulldog Power:** The No. 3 Georgia Bulldogs continued their surprising success. They remained undefeated after whomping Florida 42–7. It was such a big defeat that the Florida coach quit the day after the game! Georgia's 8–0 record had them on a path for a berth in the SEC Championship Game and a shot at the College Football Playoff.

Syracuse won this battle of orange teams!

November

SEASON HIGHLIGHTS

➜ **Wild Game in Oklahoma:** Longtime rivals No. 5 Oklahoma and No. 11 Oklahoma State lit up the scoreboard. OU QB **Baker Mayfield** set a school record with 598 passing yards. His key receiver, **Marquise Brown**, also set a new OU mark with 265 receiving yards. When the dust settled, the Sooners outlasted the Cowboys 62–52.

➜ **Top Ten Explosion!:** On November 11, the College Football Playoff standings took a beating. No. 1 Georgia was mauled by No. 10 Auburn, 40–17. It was one of the worst defeats ever for a team ranked at the top. Down at No. 3, Notre Dame had its eyes on a Playoff berth, but those hopes probably ended with a shocking 41–8 loss to No. 7

Taylor led the Badgers to a big win.

Miami. No. 6 TCU also lost, but at least they fell 38–20 to a higher-ranked team, No. 5 Oklahoma. Plus, No. 9 Washington dashed the Pac-12's Playoff hopes by losing to Stanford.

➜ **Hurricanes Hit:** The biggest surprise among the top-ranked teams was probably Miami. Once a football powerhouse, they had dropped out of the mix of elite teams. In mid-November, though, they improved to 10–0 with a 44–28 win over Virginia that included scoring the game's final 30 points. However, Miami lost the week after it reached No. 2, dooming its Playoff chances.

➜ **Badger Power:** Another undefeated team, No. 5 Wisconsin, continued its quest for a crown by beating No. 24 Michigan 24–10. The Badgers continued to have a stingy defense and a great running game, led by **Jonathan Taylor**. They needed it in part because QB **Alex Hornibrook** completed only nine passes in the game.

➜ **Down Goes 'Bama!:** No. 1 Alabama lost to No. 6 Auburn 26–14 in the Iron Bowl rivalry game. It was the Crimson Tide's first loss of the season and kept them out of the SEC Championship Game.

➜ **Thanks, Huskies!:** That's what Stanford was saying after Washington beat rival Washington State. That meant that the Cardinal would play in the Pac-12 Championship Game against USC in December. The same day Washington won, Stanford warmed up by rolling over No. 8 Notre Dame 38–20.

December
SEASON HIGHLIGHTS

CONFERENCE CHAMPIONSHIPS

AMERICAN ATHLETIC CONFERENCE
UCF 62, Memphis 55

The University of Central Florida ended up as one of only two undefeated major conference teams. They had to play overtime to do that, though. UCF intercepted a Memphis pass in the second overtime to seal the win.

ATLANTIC COAST CONFERENCE
Clemson 38, Miami 3

The Tigers earned the right to defend their 2016 national championship by crushing the Hurricanes. Ranked No. 1 entering the game, Clemson stayed there by forcing three turnovers and running for 4 TDs.

BIG TEN
Ohio State 27, Wisconsin 21

It was a big win, but it was not enough. The Buckeyes captured the Big Ten title by giving Wisconsin its first loss of the season. However, the CFP committee left Ohio State out of the final four.

BIG 12
Oklahoma 41, TCU 17

The Sooners played their way into the CFP with a big win over the Horned Frogs. Oklahoma QB **Baker Mayfield** sealed his Heisman hopes with 4 TD passes and was named the game's MVP.

Sam Darnold led the Trojans to the title.

PAC-12
USC 31, Stanford 28

A furious comeback by the Cardinal was not enough, and USC won the Pac-12 title. Its two losses on the season, though, kept it out of the final four CFP teams. Still, it was the first-ever Pac-12 title by a South Division team since the Pac-12 Championship Game began in 2011.

SEC
Georgia 28, Auburn 7

Auburn's run of big wins ended in the title game. Though they beat Georgia weeks earlier, Auburn found itself on the other end as the Bulldogs won their first SEC title since 2005.

Bowl Game Recap

College teams played 40 bowl games after the 2017 regular season. Here are some of the highlights of the most memorable games.

Army Marches In!

When Army had a chance to win the Armed Forces Bowl, it took it! Army scored a TD late against San Diego State. An extra point would have tied the game, but Army went for two and the win. **Kell Walker** carried the ball in to put Army ahead. They scored again after returning San Diego State's attempted final-play laterals to make the score 42–35. Worth noting is a great game by San Diego State's **Rashaad Penny**. He had his fifth straight 200-yard effort. His 2,248 rushing yards on the season set a new school mark and led the NCAA.

Déjà vu for TCU

In 2016, TCU set records with a 31-point comeback to win the Alamo Bowl. They came back to win again in 2017, though without a record. They were behind Stanford until the fourth quarter before taking the lead on a long punt return TD. A Stanford TD put the Cardinal back on top, but TCU bounced back again. A 33-yard field goal put them up 39–37. Then TCU intercepted a Stanford pass to clinch the surprising win.

Long Time Coming

New Mexico State had to wait 57 years and overtime to grab a bowl victory. **Larry Rose III** scored in OT and NMSU won for the first time since 1960. They beat Utah State 26–20. Both teams had kickoff-return touchdowns in the game, but Utah State missed four field goals, including one in overtime.

Purdue Harvests Win

In the Foster Farms Bowl, Purdue battled a tough Arizona team to the wire. With less

Big news! New Mexico State finally wins a bowl game!

Ohio State's defense made life tough for Sam Darnold and USC in the Cotton Bowl.

than two minutes to go, Purdue's **Anthony Mahoungou** wrestled a pass away from an Arizona defender. Then he ran to the end zone with the game-winning score. Purdue triumphed 38–35.

Cotton Crusher

Ohio State and USC have faced each other seven times in bowl games. Before 2017, all those meetings came in Rose Bowls. Because of the College Football Playoff, however, traditional bowl rivalries sometimes move. So this season, these archrivals faced off in the Cotton Bowl. OSU was disappointed at not being in the Playoffs. They took it out on the Trojans, whomping them 24–7, thanks in part to four USC turnovers. The loss was part of a disappointing 1–8 record for the Pac-12 in bowl games. The Big Ten went 7–1.

Undefeated!

Central Florida completed a perfect season with a 34–27 win over Auburn in the Peach Bowl. Defense was the key for the Knights, who held the Tigers to only 90 yards rushing on 44 attempts.

Comeback in the Outback

South Carolina trailed Michigan by 16 points in the third quarter of the Outback Bowl. But the Gamecocks had the last cluck. A 53-yard scoring pass from **Jake Bentley** to **Shi Smith** in the fourth quarter put South Carolina on top and they held on for the win.

2017 Semifinals

What a Game!

Georgia completed a huge comeback to beat Oklahoma in the Rose Bowl. The 54–48 final score was the most points ever in the game's 104 years. The teams also played the first Rose Bowl overtime. OU led 31–17 at halftime, but Georgia roared back to take a 38–31 lead. Oklahoma then scored twice to retake the lead. With less than a minute left, Georgia RB **Nick Chubb** ran in from the two to tie it up again. In the second overtime, Georgia's Lorenzo Carter blocked OU's field-goal try.

Then **Sony Michel** scampered in from 27 to send the Bulldogs to the national championship game.

Tide Rolls Again

There will be a new champ this season. Defending champ Clemson played poorly in their 24–6 Sugar Bowl loss to Alabama. The Tide defense bottled up a great Clemson offense, while also scoring on a pick-six. **Jalen Hurts** threw a pair of TD passes for Alabama. They went for their fifth national title in nine years in the championship game.

Next stop: The end zone and the National Championship Game for Michel and Georgia.

Sudden Star Lifts Tide!
2017 CHAMPIONSHIP

The biggest TV audience of the college football season got a terrific show. The College Football Playoff Championship featured two halves of great football. Georgia dominated the first half, while Alabama rolled in the second. All those fans got some extra football, as the two teams had to play overtime before Alabama came through with the biggest play of the year. The Crimson Tide gave coach **Nick Saban** his sixth national title with a shocking 26–20 win.

Georgia surprised many by shutting down 'Bama and its talented QB **Jalen Hurts** in the first half. Meanwhile, Georgia's freshman QB **Jake Fromm** led three scoring drives. The Bulldogs led 13–0 at halftime.

Then Saban surprised everyone. Maybe that's why he is now tied for most national titles all-time for a coach with the legendary **Bear Bryant**. Saban pulled Hurts and sent in freshman **Tua Tagovailoa**. It was the right move. The elusive young player inspired his team. He led them to 20 points in the second half, including two touchdown passes. Only an 80-yard bomb from Fromm to **Mecole Hardman** kept Georgia in the game.

With the score tied 20–20, Alabama's **Andy Pappanastos** missed a field goal that would have won the game.

In the first overtime, Georgia kicker

Tagovailoa came through in the clutch!

Rodrigo Blankenship thrilled his teammates by nailing a 51-yard field goal. All Georgia had to do was hold Alabama and they'd win.

The Bulldogs sacked Tagovailoa and it looked like they had sealed the win. But on the next play the surprise star floated a perfect 41-yard TD strike to **DeVonta Smith**. Game over. Tide wins. A new star is born.

We're No.1!

These are the teams that have finished at the top of the Associated Press's final rankings since the poll was first introduced in 1936.

SEASON	TEAM	RECORD	SEASON	TEAM	RECORD
2017	Alabama	13–1	1976	Pittsburgh	12–0
2016	Clemson	14–1	1975	Oklahoma	11–1
2015	Alabama	14–1	1974	Oklahoma	11–0
2014	Ohio State	14–1	1973	Notre Dame	11–0
2013	Florida State	14–0	1972	USC	12–0
2012	Alabama	13–1	1971	Nebraska	13–0
2011	Alabama	12–1	1970	Nebraska	11–0–1
2010	Auburn	14–0	1969	Texas	11–0
2009	Alabama	14–0	1968	Ohio State	10–0
2008	Florida	13–1	1967	USC	10–1
2007	LSU	12–2	1966	Notre Dame	9–0–1
2006	Florida	13–1	1965	Alabama	9–1–1
2005	Texas	13–0	1964	Alabama	10–1
2004	USC	13–0	1963	Texas	11–0
2003	USC	12–1	1962	USC	11–0
2002	Ohio State	14–0	1961	Alabama	11–0
2001	Miami (FL)	12–0	1960	Minnesota	8–2
2000	Oklahoma	13–0	1959	Syracuse	11–0
1999	Florida State	12–0	1958	LSU	11–0
1998	Tennessee	13–0	1957	Auburn	10–0
1997	Michigan	12–0	1956	Oklahoma	10–0
1996	Florida	12–1	1955	Oklahoma	11–0
1995	Nebraska	12–0	1954	Ohio State	10–0
1994	Nebraska	13–0	1953	Maryland	10–1
1993	Florida State	12–1	1952	Michigan State	9–0
1992	Alabama	13–0	1951	Tennessee	10–1
1991	Miami (FL)	12–0	1950	Oklahoma	10–1
1990	Colorado	11–1–1	1949	Notre Dame	10–0
1989	Miami (FL)	11–1	1948	Michigan	9–0
1988	Notre Dame	12–0	1947	Notre Dame	9–0
1987	Miami (FL)	12–0	1946	Notre Dame	8–0–1
1986	Penn State	12–0	1945	Army	9–0
1985	Oklahoma	11–1	1944	Army	9–0
1984	Brigham Young	13–0	1943	Notre Dame	9–1
1983	Miami (FL)	11–1	1942	Ohio State	9–1
1982	Penn State	11–1	1941	Minnesota	8–0
1981	Clemson	12–0	1940	Minnesota	8–0
1980	Georgia	12–0	1939	Texas A&M	11–0
1979	Alabama	12–0	1938	Texas Christian	11–0
1978	Alabama	11–1	1937	Pittsburgh	9–0–1
1977	Notre Dame	11–1	1936	Minnesota	7–1

NATIONAL CHAMPIONSHIP GAMES

Until the 2014 season, there was no national championship playoff system at the highest level of college football. From 1998 to 2013, the NCAA ran the Bowl Championship Series, which used computers and polls to come up with a final game that pitted the No. 1 team against the No. 2 team. The new system, called the College Football Playoff, has a panel of experts that sets up a pair of semifinal games to determine which teams play for the national title. Here are the results of BCS and College Football Playoff finals since 2000.

SEASON	TEAMS AND SCORE	SITE
2017	**Alabama 26, Georgia 20** (OT)	NEW ORLEANS, LA
2016	**Clemson 35, Alabama 31**	TAMPA, FL
2015	**Alabama 45, Clemson 40**	GLENDALE, AZ
2014	**Ohio State 42, Oregon 20**	ARLINGTON, TX
2013	**Florida State 34, Auburn 31**	PASADENA, CA
2012	**Alabama 42, Notre Dame 14**	MIAMI, FL
2011	**Alabama 21, LSU 0**	NEW ORLEANS, LA
2010	**Auburn 22, Oregon 19**	GLENDALE, AZ
2009	**Alabama 37, Texas 21**	PASADENA, CA
2008	**Florida 24, Oklahoma 14**	MIAMI, FL
2007	**LSU 38, Ohio State 24**	NEW ORLEANS, LA
2006	**Florida 41, Ohio State 14**	GLENDALE, AZ
2005	**Texas 41, USC 38**	PASADENA, CA
2004	**USC 55, Oklahoma 19**	MIAMI, FL
2003	**LSU 21, Oklahoma 14**	NEW ORLEANS, LA
2002	**Ohio State 31, Miami (FL) 24** (2 OT)	TEMPE, AZ
2001	**Miami (FL) 37, Nebraska 14**	PASADENA, CA
2000	**Oklahoma 13, Florida State 2**	MIAMI, FL

YUP! IT'S REAL GOLD!
*The United States women's hockey team
posed with their prizes after winning the gold
medal in ice hockey. It was the first gold for
the US in 20 years. Their victory capped off a
great Winter Olympics for American athletes.*

2018 WINTER OLYMPICS

Gold, Snow, and Ice

Since they began in 1896, the Olympics have brought the world together. In 2018, the world added a new wrinkle to that tradition. The Winter Games were held in South Korea, in the city of PyeongChang. South Korea's next-door country is North Korea, which is run by a scary dictator, and the two nations have been enemies for decades. But in a surprise move, North Korea offered to send athletes to the 2018 Games. A small group of athletes went and walked with South Korean athletes in the Opening Ceremony. To cap off the evening, a South Korean and North Korean hockey player carried the torch together. The togetherness might only last for those two weeks, but it was an important gesture.

Once the Games began, the athletes skated, skied, soared, snowboarded, and succeeded. One of the big winners was a country very used to snow. Norway has won more medals in Winter Olympics history than any other country. This year, Norway added 39 to its record total. Cross-country skiing is Norway's specialty, and it won 14 medals in that sport in South Korea.

Russia is often a big winner at the Winter Games. This time, the country was banned. The entire Russian team was kicked out before the Olympics began. It was a punishment for breaking rules about performance-enhancing drug use and drug testing in past Olympics. Instead, athletes from there were allowed to compete if they could prove they were drug-free. They marched under the Olympic flag as "Olympic Athletes from Russia" (OAR).

Some heroes came through as expected. In figure skating, Japan's defending gold medalist **Yuzuru Hanyu** thrilled his fans. US ski star **Mikaela Shiffrin** didn't win all the medals she tried for, but she did come home with a gold in the giant slalom. Athletes from the Netherlands, a speed-skating center, captured eight gold medals in that sport. The crowd at the Olympics got a big shock when the US men's team won curling gold. Yes . . . curling—shuffleboard on ice.

Korean athletes marched together.

Diggins (left) barely edged out a Swedish skier for gold.

nip the Swedish team in the team sprint relay by just 0.19 seconds!

Then the US women's hockey team capped off a great second week for America's Olympians. In a shootout, the team won its first gold in 20 years, beating archrival Canada.

The US women's cross-country skiers had their own surprising win. They shocked everyone by winning the first gold in American history in the sport. In the sprint relay, **Jessie Diggins** stuck out her ski to

After a slow start by America's Olympians, they rallied to put together another successful Winter Games performance. Read on for more details from the snow and ice!

Yes, it's a sport, and yes, the US men became surprise Olympic champions.

Chloe Kim, only 17, led a US gold rush in snowboarding.

USA Highlights

Snowboard Stars: Snowboarders are the music-loving rock stars of the Olympics. Many do their amazing tricks while wearing earbuds to hear their favorite tunes! The US team did really well in Korea. Teenage star **Chloe Kim**, 17, kicked things off with a win in the halfpipe. On the opposite end of the age range, **Shaun White**, 31, won his third Olympic gold in the same event. In snowboard slopestyle, another teenager, 17-year-old **Red Gerard**, surprised many experts with a win. **Jamie Anderson** won the women's event; she was the first woman ever to win two Olympic gold medals in snowboard. She also won silver in the new big air event.

▼Long Time Coming: Singles luge has been in the Olympics for 54 years. Heading into this year's Games, the US medal total for men was exactly zero. That ended with the final run by **Chris Mazder**. He slid into a silver

medal, setting off one of the most memorable and enthusiastic celebrations in years.

Short-track: See that look? ▶
That's what your face looks like after you survive a short-track speed skating race for a surprise silver medal. **John Henry Krueger** hung on while three other skaters fell.

Under Pressure: Mikaela
Shiffrin has been one of the best skiers on the planet in recent years. She was the 2017 and 2018 World Cup overall champion and the five-time slalom champ. At this Olympics, she was gunning for as many as five medals. She got her gold in the giant slalom. She was trailing after the first run, but powered down the mountain to win the event. She added a silver in the combined event.

Freestyle Skiing: Three US men
earned big medals in these events. **David Wise** and **Alex Ferreira** finished one-two in ski halfpipe. **Nick Goepper** carried home a silver in the ski slopestyle event.

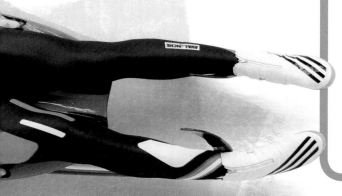

Golden Girls
In each of the previous four Olympics, Canada's women's hockey team had won the gold medal, including three victories against the US. This time, Canada shed the silver tears as the US women were back on top. The game was tied 2–2 after overtime. A shootout would determine the winner. The teams were still tied after five attempts, so the shootout went into extra time, too! **Jocelyne Lamoureux-Davidson** scored on a nifty pullback move for the US. Then goalie **Maddie Rooney** stopped **Meghan Agosta** to secure the win and the gold. It was a happy ending to an up-and-down Winter Games for the US.

Figure Skating

WOMEN'S: **Alina Zagitova** of the OAR team might have won her gold medal in practice. The day before the free skate final, she did five triple jumps in a row without stopping. Fans and her competitors were shocked. She did almost as well in the final and skated away with her first medal. Why her first? Well, she is only 15!

MEN'S: Two skaters made history in South Korea. Japan's **Yuzuru Hanyu** became the first man since 1952 to repeat as gold medalist. And American **Nathan Chen** had a first of his own: six quadruple jumps in one performance. Chen got the highest score of the event in the free skate, but his short program score was so low, he didn't even get a medal! Hanyu, meanwhile, thrilled his fans, who threw good-luck Winnie-the-Pooh dolls onto the ice in celebration!

Yuzuru Hanyu

TEAM: Canada earned the gold in the team event, and the US picked up a surprise bronze. A big reason was the performance in singles by **Mirai Nagasu**. She became the first American woman to land a triple axel at the Olympics.

Zagitova put on a golden show.

PAIRS: **Aliona Savchenko** was part of Germany's gold-medal pairs skating team. As the winning score was posted, she looked shocked. Then her face dissolved into tears of joy. Her partner, **Bruno Massot**, looked stunned, then he, too, was in tears. For Savchenko, it was her first gold medal after skating in four previous Olympics.

DANCE: **Tessa Virtue** and **Scott Moir** won the gold in ice dance. Skating last and needing a new career record to win, the top Canadian pair came through. It was their second gold medal in the event. American siblings **Maia** and **Alex Shibutani** earned the bronze.

World Stars

DUTCH TREATS: Athletes from the Netherlands dominated speed skating . . . again. In 2014, they won 23 of 26 medals. This time, they won all but one of the golds for races 1,000 meters or longer.

FINALLY!: For most of the past decade, Marcel Hirscher of Austria has been the best male skier in the world. He has won a record six consecutive World Cup overall titles, but his total of Olympic medals before Korea: 0. He righted that wrong by winning the combined event. Then he added a win in the Super-G. Did fans see the greatest ski racer ever?

HISTORIC DOUBLE: In the women's Super-G, Ester Ledecka of the Czech Republic was so shocked that she had the fastest time, she wondered if the clock was broken! She had never won a major race before, but finished ahead of the silver medalist by a razor-thin 1/100th of a second. She also won in snowboarding slalom, becoming the first athlete ever to capture gold in both types of racing.

COMEBACK KING: Martin Fourcade of France was 38 seconds behind the leader when he started the final leg of the mixed relay in biathlon. *"Pas de probléme!"* ("No problem!"), he must have said. He hit all of his rifle shots and sped past the leaders to victory. It was his third gold of the 2018 Games and his fifth ever. That made him the all-time Olympic leader, Winter or Summer, for France.

NEW MEDALS CHAMP: Norway was the medals champ in Korea. Norwegian cross-country star Marit Bjorgen became the medals champ for all time! She won five medals to reach 15 for her career. That set a new Winter Olympics medals mark.

Seeing double: Ledecka scored an Olympic first with two gold medals in different races.

Around the Games

One race, two teams, four winners: A tie in bobsled.

A Tie?

Bobsled is one of the fastest Olympic sports. Racers can reach more than 90 miles per hour on the steep track. The timing is measured in hundredths of seconds, and many races are super close. The two-man event could not get any closer. The teams from Canada and Germany each had four-run totals of 3:16.86. Both got a gold medal. Amazingly, the bronze medal winner was just 0.05 seconds behind them! That's less than an eye-blink!

Only in Short Track:

How do you get a medal for a race you were not in? And how do you finish first and get a bronze? A series of events did just that for a Netherlands team. In the women's 3,000-meter speed skating "A" final, two skaters who finished near the top were disqualified for breaking rules. In the "B" final, the Dutch team finished first. That moved them up to "third" in the other race, giving them a weird bronze.

Olympic Fashion Report:

OPENING CEREMONY: Athletes from Bermuda sported, yes, Bermuda shorts, even though the temperature was about 25 degrees. They had nothing on Pita Taufatofua, who wore only a ta'ovala (a traditional thin grass mat) as he carried the flag for Tonga.

Just watching him made us cold!

Nigeria's Olympic bobsled team broke barriers and inspired fans around the world.

CURLING: Finland broke out heart-covered pants for Valentine's Day.

FREESTYLE SKIING: Norway's Oystein Braaten won gold in ski slopestyle. Was it his skills . . . or the fact that he always wears the same pair of lucky underwear?

Winning Fans

The bobsled team from Nigeria finished 20th (out of 20) in the Olympics. That was okay. Seun Adigun, Akuoma Omeoga, and Ngozi Onwumere were the first athletes from Africa ever to take part in this super-fast sport. All three are track stars at American colleges. Inspired by other Winter Olympics rookies, they learned bobsledding less than two years ago! Every one of their races was greeted with cheers from the supportive Korean fans.

Golden smile, golden 'stache!

Mustache Man

Norway's Robert Johansson got as much attention for his awesome 'stache as for his great ski jumping. All that hair didn't affect his jumps. He got a gold in the team jumping event and bronze medals in the large and normal hill jumps.

Winter Paralympics

South Korea's Eui Hyun-sin exults!

won a medal in biathlon in Olympics or Paralympics until **Kendall Gretsch** won the sitting sprint event.

Two-Fer: **Oksana Masters** was already a Paralympic champion . . . in cycling and rowing! In Korea, she added five medals in cross-country skiing and biathlon.

Vive La France!: **Marie Bochet** earned four gold medals in standing downhill skiing events. Her French countryman, **Arthur Bauchet**, was only 17, but he won four silver medals in downhill skiing.

Local Hero: South Korea's **Eui Hyun-sin** was not expected to medal in his sitting cross-country event. Energized by the home country fans, he surprised everyone with a gold medal in the 7.5-km event.

Held a couple of weeks after the Olympics, the Winter Paralympics featured athletes with physical challenges. These amazing folks skied, skated, shot, and more, piling up medals as well as inspiration. A new record number of athletes, 567, took part in the 2018 Games. Here are some of the stars of the 2018 event.

Hockey Heroes: It took overtime, but the US men's team made the winning shot. With just 37 seconds left, **Declan Farmer** slipped a shot past the Canadian goalie to clinch his team's third straight gold medal.

An All-Time First: The United States had never

Farmer scored a golden goal for the US.

Winter Wonders

Winter Olympics Medals

COUNTRY	GOLD	SILVER	BRONZE	TOTAL
NORWAY	14	14	11	39
GERMANY	14	10	7	31
CANADA	11	8	10	29
UNITED STATES	9	8	6	23
NETHERLANDS	8	6	6	20
KOREA	5	8	4	17
OAR*	2	6	9	17
SWITZERLAND	5	6	4	15
FRANCE	5	4	6	15

*Olympic Athletes from Russia

21

That's how many nations won at least one Olympic gold medal, including six that captured only one. That does not include the Olympic Athletes from Russia, so you could also say 22 "teams" won at least one gold!

World Records!

Here are two world records that were set during the 2018 Winter Games in South Korea. More than a dozen Olympic records were also set.

–**Wu Dajing**, China, M 500-m short track speed skating, 39.584 seconds.
–Netherlands, W 3000-m relay short track speed skating 4:03.471 seconds.

UP NEXT

Here are the sites of upcoming Olympics.

2020 Summer Olympics	TOKYO, JAPAN
2022 Winter Olympics	BEIJING, CHINA
2024 Summer Olympics	PARIS, FRANCE
2026 Winter Olympics	TBA*
2028 Summer Olympics	LOS ANGELES, CA

*Will be announced in the summer of 2019.

MLB

EVERYBODY SAY "WORLD SEEEEEERIES!"
José Altuve and his Houston Astros teammates were all smiles as they posed with the 2017 World Series trophy. Houston won its first MLB championship with a dramatic seven-game win over the Los Angeles Dodgers.

Going, Going...2017!

The 2017 MLB season was the year of the home run and the super-team.

Big-league sluggers sent baseballs flying out of ballparks like never before. More homers—6,105—were hit than in any other season since big-league baseball began back in 1876. (More batters struck out, too, for the tenth straight season. But who's counting?) Baseball became a game of long ball . . . or nothing.

While the balls were flying out—or batters were walking back to the dugout—a pair of super-teams emerged. In the AL, the Houston Astros were head, shoulders, and **Dallas Keuchel**'s beard above the rest of the league. They started out 42–16 and led the AL Central by 16.5 games at the All-Star Break on their way to 101 wins.

In the NL, the Los Angeles Dodgers

Aaron Judge set the AL rookie HR record.

2017 FINAL STANDINGS

(*Playoff teams)

AL EAST		AL CENTRAL		AL WEST	
Red Sox*	93–69	Indians*	102–60	Astros*	101–61
Yankees*	91–71	Twins*	85–77	Angels	80–82
Rays	80–82	Indians	80–82	Mariners	78–84
Blue Jays	78–86	White Sox	67–95	Rangers	78–84
Orioles	75–87	Tigers	64–98	Athletics	75–87
NL EAST		**NL CENTRAL**		**NL WEST**	
Nationals*	97–65	Cubs*	92–70	Dodgers*	104–58
Marlins	77–85	Brewers	86–76	Diamondbacks*	93–69
Braves	72–90	Cardinals	83–70	Rockies*	87–75
Mets	70–92	Pirates	75–87	Padres	71–91
Phillies	66–96	Reds	68–94	Giants	64–98

The Twins made baseball's biggest comeback in 2017.

All-Star Game. In the NL East, the Washington Nationals dominated. They won by a league-high 20 games over Miami. The Dodgers were not the only NL West team with a World Series shot. Two more teams from the division, the Arizona Diamondbacks and the Colorado Rockies, also made the postseason.

Home runs flew, whiffs piled up, and everyone chased a pair of dominant teams, both of which ended up in the World Series. Sounds like a perfect recipe for a great postseason. Turn the page to see how it turned out!

were on track to set the all-time record for wins. In one stretch, they went 43–7. That was baseball's best 50-game span in 105 years. Some "experts" were calling them the best team ever. But then the Dodgers clunked through an 11-game losing streak. Still, they won 104 games, the team's most since moving to LA in 1958. It was also the most in baseball for 2017.

Even as those teams did very well, they were being chased. In the AL, the Cleveland Indians reeled off a record-setting winning streak (see page 68) as they tried to return to the World Series. The Boston Red Sox held off the hard-charging New York Yankees to win the AL East. It marked the first time in 101 years that the Sox finished in first place two years in a row. The Minnesota Twins earned the league's second wild-card berth (the Yankees secured the first) to complete a stunning turnaround. They became the first team to lose 100 games one season (they lost 103 times in 2016), and then bounce back to make the playoffs.

In the NL, the defending-champion Chicago Cubs struggled for most of the first half of the season. Would their 2016 title be a one-shot wonder? They improved a ton in the second half of the season, going a league-best 49–25 after the

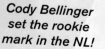

Cody Bellinger set the rookie mark in the NL!

MLB Playoffs

WILD CARD GAMES: In the AL, the Yankees fell behind 3–0 in the first. Helped by a homer from star rookie Aaron Judge, they stormed back to beat Minnesota 8–4. The Yankees' bullpen held the Twins to only one run over the final 8.2 innings. In the NL, Arizona also stormed out to an early lead. Ahead 6–0 at one point, the Diamondbacks had to hold off the Rockies. Arizona won the slugfest 11–8.

Verlander shut down the Red Sox.

ALDS
Astros 3, Red Sox 1

The Astros scored eight runs in their first two wins in this series. In Game 1, **José Altuve** became only the ninth player ever with three homers in a postseason game. Boston ace **Chris Sale** posted two losses, while Houston's **Justin Verlander**—who only joined the team on the last day in August—won a pair of games.

Yankees 3, Indians 2

New York roared back after losing the first two games to earn a surprising win over the Indians. Cleveland had won an AL-best 102 games during the regular season. They were in control after winning Game 2 by rallying from five runs down after five innings to win in the thirteenth inning. In Game 3, starter **Masahiro Tanaka** led the Yanks to a 1–0 shutout win. In Game 4, **Luis Severino** struck out nine batters, and New York tied the series with a 7–3 victory. In the series finale, shortstop **Didi Gregorius** smacked two homers and the Yankees completed their comeback with a 5–2 win in Cleveland.

NLDS
Dodgers 3, Diamondbacks 0

Arizona had LA's number during the regular season. In this series, though, the Dodgers held all the cards. They outslugged Arizona in the first two games, and then got a gem from pitcher **Yu Darvish** to complete the sweep.

Cubs 3, Nationals 2

A back-and-forth series ended with one of the most memorable playoff games in years. The Nationals jumped ahead 4–1 in Game 5 in front of their home fans. The Cubs pulled within one, and then scored four runs in the fifth inning off Nats ace **Max Scherzer**, who came on in relief. It was a wild inning, with an error, catcher's interference, and an RBI on a hit batter! Later, the Cubs got a big break when a call on a pickoff play was overturned. That shut down a Nationals' rally. Chicago held on to win the game 9–8 and the series.

ALCS
Astros 4, Yankees 3

Play at home . . . win the game. That was the theme for the ALCS between the Astros and Yankees. Houston won the first two games, each by a score of 2–1. A big reason was the performance by starter **Justin Verlander** in Game 2. The Astros won that game when **Carlos Correa** hit a walk-off RBI double. Back home at Yankee Stadium, New York called on its aces. **CC Sabathia** won 8–1 in Game 3. After the Yankees rallied to win 6–4 the next day, **Masahiro Tanaka** pitched the team to a 5–0 victory in Game 5. That put the Astros behind in the series, but with home cooking—and Verlander in Game 6— they came from behind to win their first

league title since 2005 (when they played in the National League). A clutch four-inning save from **Lance McCullers, Jr.,** usually a starter, sealed a Game 7 win.

NLCS
Dodgers 4, Cubs 1

Dodgers pitching silenced the Cubs' bats and sent LA to its first World Series since 1988. The Dodgers allowed only eight runs in the five games; their bullpen allowed none of those. In Game 2, **Justin Turner** hit a walk-off three-run homer to thrill the home fans. In Game 5, LA had a surprise hero. Super-sub **Kiké Hernandez** hit three homers and drove in seven runs to back **Clayton Kershaw** in an 11–1 victory.

Video review gave this crucial call to the Cubs.

Instant Classic!
2017 WORLD SERIES

GAME 1: Dodgers 3, Astros 1

It was 103 degrees in Los Angeles, but the hottest thing in Dodger Stadium was **Clayton Kershaw**. The megastar was finally in his first World Series game, and he came through. He allowed only three hits in seven innings. **Justin Turner** and **Chris Taylor** backed him up with home runs.

GAME 2: Astros 7, Dodgers 6 (11 inn.)

In a year that MLB set a record for homers, this wild game should not have been a surprise. The two teams set a single-game Series record with eight long balls. That wasn't even the craziest part of the night, as the teams also combined to score seven runs in the final two thrilling innings. The Astros tied the game in the ninth on a **Marwin Gonzalez** homer. Then they took a two-run lead in the top of the tenth, only to watch the Dodgers tie the game in the bottom of the inning. Then **George Springer** hit a two-run shot in the top of the eleventh. **Charlie Culberson** answered with a solo shot for LA, but the Dodgers could not push across another run. It was the most exciting back-and-forth game of the year . . . until Game 5!

GAME 3: Astros 5, Dodgers 3

Dodgers pitcher **Yu Darvish** was on a roll. He had allowed only three runs in his previous 30-plus innings. Then he got to Houston. The Astros scored four times off of him in less than two innings, and they never looked back. **Yuli Gurriel**'s homer was the big blow. Houston's bullpen didn't allow LA back in the game.

A "Springer Dinger" helped Houston win Game 2.

GAME 4: Dodgers 6, Astros 2

A wild World Series picked up the pace again in Game 4. LA's **Alex Wood** was unhittable until a home run by Springer in the sixth put up the game's first run. It was the longest no-hit string in a Series game since 1969. Houston's **Charlie Morton** was nearly as good, and the game was tied 1–1 in the ninth. That's when the Dodgers erupted for five runs to seal the victory. Rookie star **Cody Bellinger** had the big hit with an RBI double.

Correa and Spring celebrate the Astros' win!

GAME 5: Astros 13, Dodgers 12 (10 inn.)

We don't have enough room to tell the whole story of this stunning slugfest. Both teams came from behind over and over. It was too bad someone had to lose, but LA did. Houston won in the bottom of the tenth on a walk-off single by **Alex Bregman**. That run ended a back-and-forth thriller. The Astros had fallen behind early 4–0, but tied it against Dodgers ace Kershaw. Then LA jumped up 7–4 on Bellinger's three-run blast in the top of the fifth inning. Back came Houston with **José Altuve**'s matching three-run shot in the bottom of the fifth. After LA took an 8–7 lead, Houston put up four runs in the bottom of the seventh—a Springer Dinger tied the score, and then **Carlos Correa** smashed a two-run shot to put Houston up 11–8. Heading into the ninth, it was 12–9 Astros, but the fun was not over. LA got a two-run homer from **Yasiel Puig** to pull within one. Then with two strikes and two outs, Taylor lined a single that scored **Austin Barnes**. Another tie score! But even with Reliever of the Year **Kenley Jansen** on the mound in the tenth, LA could not stop Houston's 10th-inning game-winning rally. Wow! What a game!

GAME 6: Dodgers 3, Astros 1

Back in LA, the Dodgers' pitching was excellent. Starter **Rich Hill** went 4-2/3 innings, and a parade of relievers shut down Houston's offense. LA's batters did just enough against Houston ace **Verlander**. **Joc Pederson** added an insurance run with a homer in the seventh inning for the Dodgers, forcing a Game 7.

GAME 7: Astros 5, Dodgers 1

Everyone was excited about the chance for another thriller. But this one was over early. The Astros scored five runs in the first two innings and never looked back. A two-run homer by Springer, the World Series MVP, was the icing on the cake. Houston won its first World Series title.

25 The two teams set a record with that many homers in a World Series. By the way, they broke the old record of 21 after only five games!

Stat Champs

AL Hitting Leaders

52 HOME RUNS
Aaron Judge, Yankees

119 RBI
Nelson Cruz, Mariners

.346 BATTING AVERAGE
AND **204** HITS
José Altuve, Astros

34 STOLEN BASES
Whit Merrifield, Royals

Stanton was pretty good in the field, too.

NL Hitting Leaders

59 HOME RUNS AND
132 RBI
Giancarlo Stanton, Marlins

.331 BATTING AVERAGE
AND **213** HITS
Charlie Blackmon, Rockies

60 STOLEN BASES
Dee Gordon, Marlins

AL Pitching Leaders

18 WINS
Carlos Carrasco, Indians
Corey Kluber, Indians
Jason Vargas, Royals

2.25 ERA
Corey Kluber, Indians

47 SAVES
Alex Colomé, Rays

308 STRIKEOUTS
Chris Sale, Red Sox

NL Pitching Leaders

18 WINS
2.31 ERA

Clayton Kershaw, Dodgers

268 STRIKEOUTS

Max Scherzer, Nationals

41 SAVES
Greg Holland, Rockies
Kenley Jansen, Dodgers

2017 Award Winners

Kluber won his second Cy Young.

MOST VALUABLE PLAYER
AL: **José Altuve** ASTROS
NL: **Giancarlo Stanton** MARLINS

CY YOUNG AWARD
AL: **Corey Kluber** INDIANS
NL: **Max Scherzer** NATIONALS

ROOKIE OF THE YEAR
AL: **Aaron Judge** YANKEES
NL: **Cody Bellinger** DODGERS

MANAGER OF THE YEAR
AL: **Paul Molitor** TWINS
NL: **Torey Lovullo** DIAMONDBACKS

HANK AARON AWARD (OFFENSE)
AL: **José Altuve** ASTROS
NL: **Giancarlo Stanton** MARLINS

Around the Bases 2017

✳ Cleveland Rocked! The Indians put together a 22-game winning streak in 2017. That was the longest in AL history! Officially, it was also the second-longest in MLB history. The 1916 New York Giants won 26 games in a row. However, in the middle of that streak, the Giants also played a tie game! (According to the rules of the time, the game was replayed the next day, and the Giants won.)

The Indians outscored opponents 142–37 during the streak, which ended September 15 against the Royals. They set the AL record with a thrilling walk-off win over Kansas City a night earlier. **Jay Bruce** smacked the game-winning double. Cleveland rode that streak to a division title and a spot in the ALDS.

✳ Pitcher Perfect **Hailey Dawson** is only seven, but she's already tougher than most big leaguers. She was born without most of the fingers of her right hand. She now uses a cool 3D-printed hand. She's also a baseball fan. She wrote to every team and asked if she could throw out a first pitch. All of them said yes! She made it to a few in 2017, and made her biggest throw before Game 4 of the World Series (right). In 2018, she planned to complete her trip around the Major Leagues.

✳ Lots of Gloves On September 30, Detroit utility player **Andrew Romine** (left) had a very busy day. He became the fifth player ever—the first in 17 seasons—to play all nine positions in a single game. Romine played the outfield in left, center, and right for the first three innings. He moved to the infield at third, short, and second in the middle innings. In the seventh, he played catcher for the first time in his life for three batters, then went back to second base. He also pitched to one batter in the eighth (he got him out!) and ended the game at first base. Whew!

HOME RUN HEROES

The home run was the big story in MLB in 2017. More round-trippers were hit—6,105—than in any other season in league history. Along the way, all sorts of home run heroes emerged.

* **Giancarlo Stanton** of the Marlins hit 59 dingers. He was just the sixth different player in big-league history to blast that many in a season.

* **Aaron Judge** of the Yankees set a new MLB rookie record with 52 homers, beating Mark McGwire's 49 back in 1987.

* **Cody Bellinger** of the Dodgers set a new NL rookie record with 39 home runs.

* Cincinnati's **Scooter Gennett** and Arizona's **J. D. Martinez** became only the 17th and 18th players with four homers in one game. Gennett did it against the Cardinals, while Martinez sent four out of the park against the Dodgers.

* Phillies' rookie **Rhys Hoskins** smacked 18 homers in his first 34 games, an all-time high. He was the fastest ever to reach 10 homers (he needed only 17 games), too!

* Oakland rookie **Matt Olson** was nearly as good, with 24 homers in only 59 games.

* Oddly, the player who put the league over the top with the season-record 5,694th dinger was Kansas City's **Alex Gordon** . . . who only hit nine homers all season!

Scooter Gennett

Around the Bases 2018

Here are few headlines from the first half of the 2018 MLB season!

Good Start ... Bad Start:

The Boston Red Sox jumped out of the gate in a hurry. They won eight of their first nine games. They ended up with 19 wins in the month of April alone. That's the most in club history (and they've been playing since 1901!). One reason they did so well was their hot bats. The Sox tied an MLB record by hitting six grand slams in a month! Meanwhile the Los Angeles Dodgers went the other direction. After making it to Game 7 of the 2017 World Series, the boys in blue took a nosedive early in 2018. At one point, they were 16–26. That marked their worst start in team history! LA bounced back a bit above .500 in June. Would it be a be a long summer in La-La-land? Or would the Dodgers bounce back?

◀ Two-Way Star:

The Los Angeles Angels won a big prize in the 2017 offseason. Japanese star **Shohei Ohtani** chose the Halos over several other teams. Why was that such a big deal? Because Ohtani wanted to become the first player since Babe Ruth to regularly hit and pitch! Some people said it couldn't be done. Well, he hit three homers in his first two games and threw seven innings of near-perfection in his second start on the mound. Ohtani was the first player since 1919 to do that! By June, he was 4–1 and was hitting .289 with 20 RBI! Unfortunately, an arm injury cut his season short. He'll be a story to watch in the future!

O Canada! Paxton pitched a no-no!

Diamonds on the Diamond:

Some baseball players wear a lot of jewelry. You'd think it would get in their way as they run, hit, and slide. Well, in one case, you'd be right! On a hard slide into second against the Braves, Mets outfielder **Yoenis Cespedes** snapped a chain he wore around his neck. Diamonds scattered from the chain onto . . . the diamond! Cespedes and some players tried to pick up a few of the stones, but they didn't find them all.

Rally Goose!:

In a game in late May, the Detroit Tigers had a surprise guest on the field. During a rain delay, a Canadian goose landed on the field. Stadium workers tried to shoo it off as they cleaned up after the rain. The bird took off, but not far enough, and crashed into a scoreboard. Fans were worried. A vet in the stands helped make sure the bird was okay. Inspired by the bird's recovery, the Tigers rallied to win the game. They won four more in a row, and the "Rally Goose" became a regular part of the team's games.

No, No, No!:

In the first six weeks of the 2018 season, there were three no-hitters thrown in three countries! First, the **Sean Manaea** of the A's cooled off Boston's hot hitters on April 21 in Oakland. In a game played in Monterrey, Mexico, the Dodgers put together an unusual no-no over the San Diego Padres. Four Dodgers pitchers combined to keep the Pads hitless. Then on May 7, **James Paxton** of Seattle no-hit the Blue Jays in Toronto, Canada. The win was extra-special since Paxton, from British Columbia, was the first Canadian to throw a no-hitter in his home country!

With the real goose safe, a decoy duck joined Detroit.

World Series Winners

YEAR	WINNER	RUNNER-UP	SCORE*	YEAR	WINNER	RUNNER-UP	SCORE*
2017	Houston Astros	Los Angeles Dodgers	4-3	1989	Oakland Athletics	San Francisco Giants	4-0
2016	Chicago Cubs	Cleveland Indians	4-3	1988	Los Angeles Dodgers	Oakland Athletics	4-1
2015	Kansas City Royals	New York Mets	4-1	1987	Minnesota Twins	St. Louis Cardinals	4-3
2014	San Francisco Giants	Kansas City Royals	4-3	1986	New York Mets	Boston Red Sox	4-3
2013	Boston Red Sox	St. Louis Cardinals	4-2	1985	Kansas City Royals	St. Louis Cardinals	4-3
2012	San Francisco Giants	Detroit Tigers	4-0	1984	Detroit Tigers	San Diego Padres	4-1
2011	St. Louis Cardinals	Texas Rangers	4-3	1983	Baltimore Orioles	Philadelphia Phillies	4-1
2010	San Francisco Giants	Texas Rangers	4-1	1982	St. Louis Cardinals	Milwaukee Brewers	4-3
2009	New York Yankees	Philadelphia Phillies	4-2	1981	Los Angeles Dodgers	New York Yankees	4-2
2008	Philadelphia Phillies	Tampa Bay Rays	4-1	1980	Philadelphia Phillies	Kansas City Royals	4-2
2007	Boston Red Sox	Colorado Rockies	4-0	1979	Pittsburgh Pirates	Baltimore Orioles	4-3
2006	St. Louis Cardinals	Detroit Tigers	4-1	1978	New York Yankees	Los Angeles Dodgers	4-2
2005	Chicago White Sox	Houston Astros	4-0	1977	New York Yankees	Los Angeles Dodgers	4-2
2004	Boston Red Sox	St. Louis Cardinals	4-0	1976	Cincinnati Reds	New York Yankees	4-0
2003	Florida Marlins	New York Yankees	4-2	1975	Cincinnati Reds	Boston Red Sox	4-3
2002	Anaheim Angels	San Francisco Giants	4-3	1974	Oakland Athletics	Los Angeles Dodgers	4-1
2001	Arizona Diamondbacks	New York Yankees	4-3	1973	Oakland Athletics	New York Mets	4-3
2000	New York Yankees	New York Mets	4-1	1972	Oakland Athletics	Cincinnati Reds	4-3
1999	New York Yankees	Atlanta Braves	4-0	1971	Pittsburgh Pirates	Baltimore Orioles	4-3
1998	New York Yankees	San Diego Padres	4-0	1970	Baltimore Orioles	Cincinnati Reds	4-1
1997	Florida Marlins	Cleveland Indians	4-3	1969	New York Mets	Baltimore Orioles	4-1
1996	New York Yankees	Atlanta Braves	4-2	1968	Detroit Tigers	St. Louis Cardinals	4-3
1995	Atlanta Braves	Cleveland Indians	4-2	1967	St. Louis Cardinals	Boston Red Sox	4-3
1993	Toronto Blue Jays	Philadelphia Phillies	4-2	1966	Baltimore Orioles	Los Angeles Dodgers	4-0
1992	Toronto Blue Jays	Atlanta Braves	4-2	1965	Los Angeles Dodgers	Minnesota Twins	4-3
1991	Minnesota Twins	Atlanta Braves	4-3	1964	St. Louis Cardinals	New York Yankees	4-3
1990	Cincinnati Reds	Oakland Athletics	4-0	1963	Los Angeles Dodgers	New York Yankees	4-0

* Score is represented in games played.

YEAR	WINNER	RUNNER-UP	SCORE*
1962	New York Yankees	San Francisco Giants	4-3
1961	New York Yankees	Cincinnati Reds	4-1
1960	Pittsburgh Pirates	New York Yankees	4-3
1959	Los Angeles Dodgers	Chicago White Sox	4-2
1958	New York Yankees	Milwaukee Braves	4-3
1957	Milwaukee Braves	New York Yankees	4-3
1956	New York Yankees	Brooklyn Dodgers	4-3
1955	Brooklyn Dodgers	New York Yankees	4-3
1954	New York Giants	Cleveland Indians	4-0
1953	New York Yankees	Brooklyn Dodgers	4-2
1952	New York Yankees	Brooklyn Dodgers	4-3
1951	New York Yankees	New York Giants	4-2
1950	New York Yankees	Philadelphia Phillies	4-0
1949	New York Yankees	Brooklyn Dodgers	4-1
1948	Cleveland Indians	Boston Braves	4-2
1947	New York Yankees	Brooklyn Dodgers	4-3
1946	St. Louis Cardinals	Boston Red Sox	4-3
1945	Detroit Tigers	Chicago Cubs	4-3
1944	St. Louis Cardinals	St. Louis Browns	4-2
1943	New York Yankees	St. Louis Cardinals	4-1
1942	St. Louis Cardinals	New York Yankees	4-1
1941	New York Yankees	Brooklyn Dodgers	4-1
1940	Cincinnati Reds	Detroit Tigers	4-3
1939	New York Yankees	Cincinnati Reds	4-0
1938	New York Yankees	Chicago Cubs	4-0
1937	New York Yankees	New York Giants	4-1
1936	New York Yankees	New York Giants	4-2
1935	Detroit Tigers	Chicago Cubs	4-2
1934	St. Louis Cardinals	Detroit Tigers	4-3
1933	New York Giants	Washington Senators	4-1

YEAR	WINNER	RUNNER-UP	SCORE*
1932	New York Yankees	Chicago Cubs	4-0
1931	St. Louis Cardinals	Philadelphia Athletics	4-3
1930	Philadelphia Athletics	St. Louis Cardinals	4-2
1929	Philadelphia Athletics	Chicago Cubs	4-1
1928	New York Yankees	St. Louis Cardinals	4-0
1927	New York Yankees	Pittsburgh Pirates	4-0
1926	St. Louis Cardinals	New York Yankees	4-3
1925	Pittsburgh Pirates	Washington Senators	4-3
1924	Washington Senators	New York Giants	4-3
1923	New York Yankees	New York Giants	4-2
1922	New York Giants	New York Yankees	4-0
1921	New York Giants	New York Yankees	5-3
1920	Cleveland Indians	Brooklyn Robins	5-2
1919	Cincinnati Reds	Chicago White Sox	5-3
1918	Boston Red Sox	Chicago Cubs	4-2
1917	Chicago White Sox	New York Giants	4-2
1916	Boston Red Sox	Brooklyn Robins	4-1
1915	Boston Red Sox	Philadelphia Phillies	4-1
1914	Boston Braves	Philadelphia Athletics	4-0
1913	Philadelphia Athletics	New York Giants	4-1
1912	Boston Red Sox	New York Giants	4-3
1911	Philadelphia Athletics	New York Giants	4-2
1910	Philadelphia Athletics	Chicago Cubs	4-1
1909	Pittsburgh Pirates	Detroit Tigers	4-3
1908	Chicago Cubs	Detroit Tigers	4-1
1907	Chicago Cubs	Detroit Tigers	4-0
1906	Chicago White Sox	Chicago Cubs	4-2
1905	New York Giants	Philadelphia Athletics	4-1
1903	Boston Americans	Pittsburgh Pirates	5-3

Note: 1904 not played because NL-champion Giants refused to play; 1994 not played due to MLB work stoppage.

SOCCER

SINGING IN THE RAIN!

Minutes after France captured its second World Cup, a rainstorm soaked the stadium in Moscow. The celebrating French players didn't mind a bit! They would have waded into the ocean for a chance to hold the World Cup trophy. Catch up on all the action on the following pages!

Best World Cup Ever?

Was this the best World Cup tournament ever? After watching more than a month of awesome action, great goals, and stunning saves, many fans were saying the answer was **yes**! France won its second World Cup, but they were the only "big-name" country to make the final four. The top soccer nations in the world faced a rising tide of good new teams. Of course, former soccer powers such as Italy and the Netherlands didn't even earn a place in Russia, where the World Cup was held. Once the games began, there were plenty of surprising upsets, along with possibly the final World Cup games for two great stars.

Portgual's **Cristiano Ronaldo** (left) could not lead his team past the Round of 16. Argentina's **Lionel Messi** also saw his team lose in that round. Both will probably be too old to play in the 2022 World Cup. They have had marvelous careers, but will miss putting the biggest trophy of all on their shelves.

This World Cup did feature more scoring than usual. Only one game ended at 0–0. This was the first World Cup tournament in which each team scored two goals in at least one game. Fans saw a lot of exciting finishes, too. Nine winning goals were scored in the 90th minute or later! While some top teams were falling, others were finding new life. England came in with big hopes and made them pay off with a semifinal spot. Croatia proved to be the comeback kings. France not only won the Cup, but showed off a great young team that might have its eye on 2022 already! There were also big upsets and surprising results . . . dominant teams and superstars . . . and tears of joy at the end. You can catch up on all the action in our special section starting on page 80.

UEFA Champions League

The World Cup was not the only big soccer event in 2018. The annual UEFA Champions League pits the top club teams in Europe against each other in a massive playoff. The winner is considered the best team in Europe, if not the world. Once again in 2018, it was Real Madrid. Led by the amazing **Cristiano Ronaldo**, Real became the first team to twice win three Champions Leagues in a row—they also did it from 1956–60. In the 2018 final, the story was not Ronaldo, however. **Gareth Bale** scored the go-ahead goal on a remarkable bicycle kick (right) that stunned the fans and the opponent, Liverpool. Bale scored a second goal from more than 30 yards out to seal the 3–1 victory.

THORNS WIN NWSL

The Women's World Cup will not be held until the summer of 2019. In the meantime, the top players in the world got their kicks in the National Women's Soccer League. The Portland Thorns captured their second NWSL championship. They beat the North Carolina Courage 1–0 on a goal by US national team player Lindsey Horan (in red). North Carolina had the regular season's best record, but could not bring home the final trophy. It was Portland's second title; they also won in 2013.

The biggest winner in 2017 might have been the league itself, however. The NWSL played its fifth season, making it the longest-lasting US women's pro league. A national TV contract has helped, along with a much higher level of play. Ten teams are in the league, playing a 24-game season. If you haven't seen an NWSL game yet, check one out! It's great soccer!

World Cup Highlights

Home Cooking

Russia was the host of the tournament, so they got an automatic bid to play. They came in as the lowest-ranked team but did not play like it. They swamped Saudi Arabia 5–0 in the opening game. Then they beat Egypt 3–1 to earn a spot in the second round. Things got even better when they shocked Spain in a penalty-kick shootout. A quarterfinal loss to Croatia ended a great run for the home team.

Ronaldo Ties Spain!

The great **Cristiano Ronaldo** scored a hat trick to match Spain's three goals in one of the most exciting games of the first round. Spain led 3–2 late in the game when Ronaldo stood over a free kick. He curled in a beauty around the wall for a tie that played a big part in helping Portugal move to the next round. Ronaldo also became the fourth player ever to score in four World Cups.

Mexican goalie Guillermo Ochoa (orange) played a big role in Mexico's upset of Germany.

QUARTERFINALS

FRANCE 2, URUGUAY 0
France knocked out the last non-European team with solid defense. They had to be solid against the great skills of **Luis Suarez**. Goals by **Raphaël Varane** and **Antoine Griezmann** were the difference.

ENGLAND 2, SWEDEN 0
The English team thrilled fans at home by advancing. Their semifinal spot was the farthest the team had gone since winning it all in 1966. **Harry Maguire** and **Deli Alli** scored for the Three Lions.

BELGIUM 2, BRAZIL 1 ▶▶▶
In one of the tournament's best games, Belgium's strong defense kept high-scoring Brazil quiet. An early own goal by Brazil put them in a hole they could not dig out of. The marvelous **Kevin de Bruyne** (in red) slammed home the game-winner for Belgium.

CROATIA 2, RUSSIA 2 (4-3 in PKs)
This game ended in a penalty-kick shootout after both teams scored in extra time. A huge save by Croatian goalie **Danijel Subasi** helped his team move on.

Viking Attack!
Iceland was the smallest country ever to make it to the World Cup. Argentina has won two World Cups and features the great **Lionel Messi**. But Messi missed a penalty kick in this game and Iceland earned a surprising 1–1 tie.

What Happened to Germany?
In one of the biggest upsets of the first round, Mexico beat Germany 1–0. The World Cup defending champion looked slow and out of sorts. (In that game, Mexico's **Rafa Marquez** became the third player to appear in five World Cups.) Germany won their second game on a last-minute free kick by **Toni Kroos**. Then in a must-win game against South Korea, they could not score. A 2-0 loss sent the 2014 winners home early!

Set Pieces
Soccer fans heard those words over and over. Goals scored on free kicks, corner kicks, and penalty kicks came faster than ever before. Teams spend many hours practicing set pieces. The work paid off as goals poured in from great curving kicks to headers from high-flying players. Watch for more time on corners and free kicks at your next AYSO practice!

Croatia's Mario Mandzukic (17) ended England's World Cup dream with this goal in extra time.

World Cup Semifinals

Croatia 2, England 1

The small nation of Croatia took a huge step toward a championship with another come-from-behind win. They made history by becoming the first team with three extra-time victories. England scored first on a great free kick (set pieces again!) by **Kevin Trippier**. **Ivan Perisic** tied the score to force extra time. With about 12 minutes to go before penalties, **Mario Mandzukic** pounced on a loose ball and slammed home the game-winner.

France 1, Belgium 0

France had impressed fans with a great offense throughout the tournament. For this game, they called on their great defense. Belgium had been having its way with every opponent, but they could not dent the French wall. **Samuel Umtiti** bounced in a header for France off a corner kick in the second half. Then France defended attack after attack. Goalie **Hugo Lloris**, the French captain, was excellent in the nets, making several key saves.

Video Referee

For the first time, the World Cup referees could use video to review key plays. The video assistant referee (VAR) worked in a studio. If he saw a tricky call, he would alert the match ref. That official then could run to the sidelines to look at a TV screen. In all, seven penalty kicks were awarded thanks to VAR, including a key one in the final.

World Cup Final

This was a battle of favorite vs. underdog. France entered the game as one of the youngest teams, but also as one of the most talented. They had beaten top teams like Brazil and Belgium. Croatia has only been a country since 1998 and was making its first appearance in the final game. They had shown great heart in coming from behind again and again.

Croatia made the first mistake of the game. **Mario Mandzukic**, the hero of the semifinal, headed in an own goal, the first-ever in a World Cup final. **Ivan Perisic** tied the score soon after with a great left-footed shot.

A few minutes later, Perisic was caught by TV using his hand to deflect a shot. The VAR (see box) was used and France got a penalty kick. **Antoine Griezmann** buried it.

France's Pogba blasts a key second-half goal.

In the second half, France poured it on. Midfielder **Paul Pogba** slammed home a shot from about 20 yards out. Then young star player **Kylian Mbappé** whipped a shot past the Croatian goalie to make it 4–1. Mbappé, 19, was the first teenager to score in a World Cup final since the great **Pelé** scored two goals in 1958 at the age of 17. A mistake by French goalie **Hugo Lloris** that made the score 4–2 was not enough. France held on to win its second World Cup and first since 1998.

Didier Deschamps made history by becoming the third man to be both captain of a World Cup winner and the coach of one. As a midfielder, he had led France to that first Cup in 1998.

WORLD CUP AWARDS

GOLDEN BALL (TOP PLAYER)
Luka Modric, Croatia

GOLDEN BOOT (TOP GOAL SCORER)
Harry Kane, England

GOLDEN GLOVES (TOP GOALIE)
Thibaut Courtois, Belgium

SILVER BALL (TOP YOUNG PLAYER)
Kylian Mbappé, France

2017 Major League Soccer

The biggest story in MLS 2017 was powerhouse FC Toronto. After losing the 2016 MLS Cup on penalty kicks, they were taking no chances in 2017. Toronto already had US stars **Michael Bradley** and **Jozy Altidore**. Then they added several good young players and turned into the league's top team. They easily won the Supporters' Shield with the best regular-season record and a new MLS record 69 points. They capped off their amazing season with a thrilling 2–0 MLS Cup championship in front of their loyal fans.

In other news, two new teams joined MLS in 2017. The Atlanta United got their first goal ever in their opening game, courtesy of **Yamil Asad**. It didn't lead to their first win, though. That didn't come until their second game, which was a memorable contest played in a snowstorm against the other new team, the Minnesota United.

Atlanta would end up making the playoffs, while Minnesota struggled and did not. Atlanta also set a new MLS record for attendance. The team drew 819,404 fans to its home games. One of them, a late-season showdown with Toronto, also set the single-game record of 71,874.

As always, some big international stars joined MLS. One of the biggest was German national team star **Bastian Schweinsteiger**. He announced his arrival by scoring in the first half of his first game for the Chicago Fire. (Former Manchester United star **Wayne Rooney** was a mid-2018 addition for D.C. United.)

After Toronto put up its record-breaking 69 points, the team struggled in the playoffs at first. They held on to advance past NYCFC. Then they beat the Columbus Crew in the conference final. In the West, defending champ Seattle reached the conference final, where they knocked off the surprising Houston Dynamo.

At the MLS Cup, **Jozy Altidore** scored in the second half before a last-minute goal made the final score 2–0 Toronto. O Canada indeed!

Altidore's goal put Toronto in front at the MLS Cup.

Nothing new here—just another goal for the record-setting Manchester City team.

Premier League

Manchester City dominated the Premier League as no team ever has. When the dust settled and the trophy was raised, they had rewritten the team record books. The team poured in points and piled up wins better than any team yet.

97 Most points in a season
(3 points for a win, 1 point for a tie)

31 Most victories in a season

105 Most goals in a season

The boys in light blue were led by Belgian star **Kevin de Bruyne** and **Vincent Kompany**, English players including defender **Dwight Stones** and goalie **Joe Hart**, and high-scoring Argentine star **Sergio Aguero**.

In other Premier League news, **Harry Kane** of Tottenham Hotspur set an interesting record. With a total of 56 goals scored in 2017 between his club and his English national team, Kane broke the record of 54 set by **Lionel Messi**, who scored his for FC Barcelona and Argentina.

Marvelous Mo!

Man City got the top trophy, but Liverpool had something to celebrate, too. The team's top striker, **Mo Salah** from Egypt, scored 32 goals in the team's 38 games. That set a new single-season record for the league. Salah won the scoring race over **Harry Kane**, who had won the previous two seasons. Not surprisingly, Salah was also named Player of the Year.

Stat Stuff

MAJOR LEAGUE SOCCER
CHAMPIONS

2017 FC Toronto
2016 Seattle Sounders
2015 Portland Timbers
2014 Los Angeles Galaxy
2013 Sporting Kansas City
2012 Los Angeles Galaxy
2011 Los Angeles Galaxy
2010 Colorado Rapids
2009 Real Salt Lake
2008 Columbus Crew
2007 Houston Dynamo
2006 Houston Dynamo
2005 Los Angeles Galaxy
2004 D.C. United
2003 San Jose Earthquakes
2002 Los Angeles Galaxy
2001 San Jose Earthquakes
2000 Kansas City Wizards
1999 D.C. United
1998 Chicago Fire
1997 D.C. United
1996 D.C. United

UEFA CHAMPIONS
LEAGUE

The Champions League pits the best against the best. The top club teams from the members of UEFA (the Union of European Football Associations) face off in a months-long tournament.

2018 Real Madrid SPAIN
2017 Real Madrid SPAIN
2016 Real Madrid SPAIN
2015 FC Barcelona SPAIN
2014 Real Madrid SPAIN
2013 Bayern Munich GERMANY
2012 Chelsea FC ENGLAND
2011 FC Barcelona SPAIN
2010 Inter (Milan) ITALY
2009 FC Barcelona SPAIN
2008 Manchester United ENGLAND
2007 AC Milan ITALY
2006 FC Barcelona SPAIN
2005 Liverpool FC ENGLAND
2004 FC Porto PORTUGAL
2003 AC Milan ITALY
2002 Real Madrid SPAIN

WORLD CUP WINNERS

YEAR	CHAMPION	LOCATION
2018	**France**	Russia
2014	**Germany**	Brazil
2010	**Spain**	South Africa
2006	**Italy**	Germany
2002	**Brazil**	South Korea/Japan
1998	**France**	France
1994	**Brazil**	United States
1990	**West Germany**	Italy
1986	**Argentina**	Mexico
1982	**Italy**	Spain
1978	**Argentina**	Argentina
1974	**West Germany**	West Germany
1970	**Brazil**	Mexico
1966	**England**	England
1962	**Brazil**	Chile
1958	**Brazil**	Sweden
1954	**West Germany**	Switzerland
1950	**Uruguay**	Brazil
1938	**Italy**	France
1934	**Italy**	Italy
1930	**Uruguay**	Uruguay

EYES ON THE PRIZE

As the clocked ticked down at the end of the NCAA women's championship game, all eyes were on the ball. Notre Dame's Arike Ogunbowale (bottom right in blue) had just launched it from the corner. As the clock ticked to 0.1, the ball went in the basket and the Irish were champs!

COLLEGE BASKETBALL

Basketball or Roller Coaster?

Like a basketball being dribbled up and down, the 2017–18 men's college hoops season saw more than its fair share of bounces. There was not a really dominant team. Villanova, Virginia, Duke, Purdue, and Michigan all took turns at the top, but none really pulled away.

Young had a historic season double.

Perhaps the most famous player was Oklahoma freshman **Trae Young**. He led the nation in both scoring (27.4 points per game average) and assists (8.7 assists per game). He was the first player since 1983, when assists became an official NCAA stat, to accomplish that feat. As good as Young was, though, his Sooners went home "too soon" in the NCAA tournament.

Freshmen like Young were a big part of the story of the season. That's not surprising, though, in these days of "one and done." That phrase refers to the way that top high school players stick around for only one season of college, then hop to the pros. In 2018, three freshmen made the Associated Press All-America team, a first in the 70-year history of the award. The top trio included Young, of course. He was joined by **Deandre Ayton** of Arizona and **Marvin Bagley III** of Duke. All three are now on NBA rosters.

Some things were not new, however. Kansas won its amazing 13th straight Big 12 season title. Virginia continued to be a top team, but it hit a huge speed bump in the tournament (see page 93!). Duke was once again in the mix. Along the way, its coach, **Mike Krzyzewski** (pronounced "sha-SHEFF-ski"), set a new record with his 1,099th career victory. That passed late Tennessee women's coach **Pat Summitt** for the most ever. Nice going, Coach K!

The up-and-down men's season continued in the NCAA tournament. Upsets popped up all over the bracket. In the women's tournament, a new champ was crowned on an historic shot. Read on for all the details!

AWARD WINNERS

JOHN R. WOODEN AWARD
NAISMITH AWARD

Jalen Brunson/VILLANOVA
A'ja Wilson/SOUTH CAROLINA

COACH OF THE YEAR

Jay Wright/VILLANOVA
Muffet McGraw/NOTRE DAME

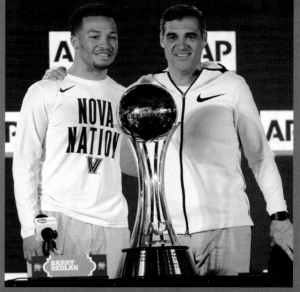

Brunson and Wright both earned top honors.

FINAL MEN'S TOP 10
USA Today Coaches Poll

1. Villanova
2. Michigan
3. Kansas
4. Duke
5. Virginia
6. Texas Tech
7. Loyola-Chicago
8. Xavier
9. Purdue
10. Gonzaga

FINAL WOMEN'S TOP 10
USA Today Coaches Poll

1. Notre Dame
2. Mississippi State
3. Connecticut
4. Louisville
5. Oregon
6. South Carolina
7. UCLA
8. Oregon State
9. Baylor
10. Texas

43

That is how many different schools appeared at least once in the AP Top 25 rankings in 2017–2018. Amazingly, Loyola-Chicago's first appearance was AFTER the season. Why? The answer is on page 94.

2017-18 Hoops
SEASON HIGHLIGHTS

5 on 3?: In a November game, Alabama almost pulled off the greatest upset of all time. After a fight in the second half of a game against Minnesota, all of Alabama's reserves were ejected for leaving the bench. Then a Crimson Tide player fouled out and another sprained an ankle. That left just three 'Bama players on the court against Minnesota's five for the final 10-plus minutes of a game in which Alabama trailed by 13 points. Amazingly, the Crimson Tide outscored the Gophers 30–22 the rest of the way. It was not enough to win, however, except for fans of "the old college try."

What's a Wofford?: That's what North Carolina was asking after a December game. UNC is one of college basketball's most famous programs. The Tar Heels have won six national titles. Wofford College, a small school in South Carolina . . . hasn't. But No. 5 North Carolina found out who Wofford is in a big way. The Terriers shocked the Heels 79–75 and ended Carolina's 23-game home winning streak.

Half-Court Crusher: USC thought it had pulled off a comeback win over Stanford in January when it scored with 1.7 seconds left. But that was enough time for the Cardinal's **Daejon Davis** to take an inbounds pass and one dribble. He heaved up a shot from behind the half-court line . . . that went in! The three-pointer gave Stanford a shocking 77–76 win.

A Good Week: St. John's had a pretty good week in early February. Through January, the Big East team had a losing record that included an 11-game losing streak. Then the Red Storm pulled off a huge upset by beating No. 4–ranked Duke. They topped that by handing No. 1–ranked Villanova one of its only four losses on the year. Stats showed that it was the first time a team with a conference record of 0–10 had topped a No. 1 team!

Wofford smothered No. 5 North Carolina.

NCAA Tournament

16 OVER 1!: After this game, everything else moved to second place . . . even the eventual champion! For the first time ever, a No. 16 seed shocked a No. 1 seed. Until this game, the 1 vs. 16 record was 135–0! The University of Maryland, Baltimore County (UMBC) Retrievers not only beat the top-seeded Virginia Cavaliers, they crushed them. Virginia was cold as ice, while UMBC poured in threes and dunks. Even crazier, it was tied 21–21 at halftime! In the second half, UMBC ran away with the game, finishing 20 points ahead (74–54) of a team that had lost only two games all season. Many experts said it was the biggest upset in college hoops history. Wow!

LUCKY 13S!: In a tournament packed with surprises, two No. 13 teams pulled off big upsets. Buffalo crushed Pac-12 power Arizona 89–68. Then Marshall shocked the Wichita State Shockers 81–75.

THE PAC-ZERO: The Pac-12 had a horrible NCAA tournament. First, USC was somehow left out of the final 68 teams even though the school had finished second in its conference. Once play began, nationally ranked UCLA, Arizona, and Arizona State all lost their first games.

UMBC rose to an historic win.

WHAT A COMEBACK!: Cincinnati was cruising. In the Bearcats' second-round game against Nevada, they led by 22 points! Time to celebrate? Not so fast. The Wolfpack roared back, closing the gap little by little. With 9.1 seconds left, they scored to finally take the lead! Nevada won 75–73. Its victory was the second-biggest comeback in NCAA tournament history!

More NCAA Tournament

A great run led Loyola to a spot in the final Top 10.

LOYOLA ROLLS!

Other than the 16 over 1 upset, the play of Loyola-Chicago was the biggest story of the tournament. Seeded No. 11, the Ramblers had not won an NCAA tournament game since 1963 . . . when they were the champions! In 2018, they shocked No. 6 Miami in the first game on a buzzer-beater. In the next round, the Ramblers got a great bounce on a shot with 3.6 seconds left. It went in, and they had their second upset, this time over Tennessee. In the Sweet 16, they beat another surprise team, No. 7 seed Nevada. Then, in the Elite Eight, Loyola crushed Kansas State 78–62. Loyola tied the record for highest seed to make the Final Four.

BUZZER BEATERS!

The tournament is always packed with close games and last-second shots. Here are three of the most memorable from 2018:

* Michigan had to move the ball the length of the court with 3.6 seconds left, down by two points. **Jordan Poole** *(right)* launched a 30-foot, three-point prayer that was answered. At the buzzer, the Wolverines beat Houston 64–63.

* The Gonzaga and UNC-Greensboro game didn't end on a buzzer-beater, but close. A Zags' three-pointer put them up with 20.8 seconds left, and they held on for a big win.

* Houston avoided an upset by scoring a layup with 1.1 seconds left. It provided the winning points in a 67–65 victory over San Diego State.

THE MOP! That stands for Most Outstanding Player, an award given to one athlete from a Final Four team. Not surprisingly, a player from the winning team has won it just about every time. In 2018, it was 'Nova's **Donte DiVincenzo** *(left, in white)*. In the semifinal, he had 15 points, but he really went to town in the final. His 31 points led all scorers and led to a Wildcats title.

SEMIFINALS

Loyola's Cinderella season ended with a national semifinal loss to Michigan. German-born **Moritz Wagner** of Michigan had 24 points and 15 rebounds. He was the first player since 1983 with at least 20 points and 15 boards in a national semifinal. To cap off his day, he led his team with three steals! In the other semi, Villanova continued its tournament-long roll. Using a record-tying 13 first half three-pointers, the Wildcats rolled to a 16-point win over fellow No. 1 seed Kansas.

CHAMPIONSHIP GAME

The Wildcats from 'Nova, who were the NCAA champs in 2016, looked very strong heading into the final. A tournament that had more upsets than usual ended with a dominant win by a top team. Villanova crushed Michigan 79–62. The surprise hero was **Donte DiVincenzo**. Usually a part-time player, he was so hot he played most of the game. He scored 18 of his team's first 32 points. Only one other Wildcats' shooter even cracked double figures (**Mikal Bridges** with 19). The victory gave Villanova its second title in three seasons, joining the trophy it won in 2016.

V is for Villanova . . . and victory! The Wildcats celebrated their second title in three years.

NCAA Women's Hoops

For most of the regular season, it looked like the powerful Connecticut team would reclaim its spot at the top. After all, its 111-game winning streak had ended in the 2017 national semifinal. During the 2017–18 regular season, the team was undefeated . . . again. But that's why they play the tournament!

In the women's brackets, the number 11 was a good spot to be seeded. Three teams given that seeding pulled off big upsets.

Creighton beat No. 6 Iowa. **Jaylyn Agnew** led the way with 24 points.

Buffalo forged another 11 upset. The Bulls crushed South Florida in the opening round 102–79. That was the second-highest point total of the round behind (you guessed it) UConn. The Huskies piled up 140 points in an 88-point rout of St. Francis. Buffalo did Creighton one better, though, going on to upset No. 3 Florida State in the next round.

A third No. 11 seed, Central Michigan, matched Buffalo. The Chippewas surprised LSU in the opening round, then stunned No. 3 Ohio State 95–78. The Buckeyes had been a top-10 team all season, but Central Michigan had their number.

After all the upsets were over, though, things stayed in order. The top teams dodged the upsets, and the Final Four featured all four No. 1 seeds. And then things got really interesting!

Cassie Breen helped Central Michigan to big upsets.

Ogunbowale was the buzzer-beating, high-leaping, crowd-pleasing Final Four hero.

SEMIFINALS

Mississippi State was used to shocking tournament wins. The Bulldogs stopped UConn's winning streak in 2017. In an overtime semifinal win over Louisville in 2018, they nearly matched that excitement. They tied the game with 5 seconds left to force OT. In the extra period, they continued to roll and put up a 10-point win.

In the other semifinal, it was a battle of titans. Undefeated UConn faced three-loss Notre Dame. A hard-fought, back-and-forth game came down to one shot . . . and ND made it. First, though, the Huskies had to rally from five points down with 21.3 seconds left to force overtime. The extra period was tied with 13 seconds left. On the game's final play, Notre Dame's **Arike Ogunbowale** rose up above a crowd of players to hit the game-winning shot!

CHAMPIONSHIP GAME

Did you see how that last semifinal game ended? Well, get ready to hit the repeat button! Notre Dame was behind Mississippi State by 13 points at halftime. A furious rally left the two teams very close in the final moments of the fourth quarter. Then Notre Dame tied the score on a long three, and it looked like this game would also go overtime. But that's when Ogunbowale worked her magic . . . again. Going up against a taller opponent, she went to the corner and lofted a high, arcing three-point attempt. It went in with 0.1 seconds remaining! Start the celebration! The Fighting Irish earned their first title since 2001. Fans could not remember a player, man or woman, pulling off similar back-to-back game-winners, certainly not in such crucial games.

NCAA Champs!

MEN'S DIVISION I

2018 **Villanova**	1999 **Connecticut**	1980 **Louisville**
2017 **North Carolina**	1998 **Kentucky**	1979 **Michigan State**
2016 **Villanova**	1997 **Arizona**	1978 **Kentucky**
2015 **Duke**	1996 **Kentucky**	1977 **Marquette**
2014 **Connecticut**	1995 **UCLA**	1976 **Indiana**
2013 **Louisville**	1994 **Arkansas**	1975 **UCLA**
2012 **Kentucky**	1993 **North Carolina**	1974 **NC State**
2011 **Connecticut**	1992 **Duke**	1973 **UCLA**
2010 **Duke**	1991 **Duke**	1972 **UCLA**
2009 **North Carolina**	1990 **UNLV**	1971 **UCLA**
2008 **Kansas**	1989 **Michigan**	1970 **UCLA**
2007 **Florida**	1988 **Kansas**	1969 **UCLA**
2006 **Florida**	1987 **Indiana**	1968 **UCLA**
2005 **North Carolina**	1986 **Louisville**	1967 **UCLA**
2004 **Connecticut**	1985 **Villanova**	1966 **Texas Western**
2003 **Syracuse**	1984 **Georgetown**	1965 **UCLA**
2002 **Maryland**	1983 **NC State**	1964 **UCLA**
2001 **Duke**	1982 **North Carolina**	1963 **Loyola (Illinois)**
2000 **Michigan State**	1981 **Indiana**	1962 **Cincinnati**

1961 **Cincinnati**
1960 **Ohio State**
1959 **California**
1958 **Kentucky**
1957 **North Carolina**
1956 **San Francisco**
1955 **San Francisco**
1954 **La Salle**

1953 **Indiana**
1952 **Kansas**
1951 **Kentucky**
1950 **City Coll. of NY**
1949 **Kentucky**
1948 **Kentucky**
1947 **Holy Cross**
1946 **Oklahoma A&M**

1945 **Oklahoma A&M**
1944 **Utah**
1943 **Wyoming**
1942 **Stanford**
1941 **Wisconsin**
1940 **Indiana**
1939 **Oregon**

WOMEN'S DIVISION I

2018 **Notre Dame**
2017 **South Carolina**
2016 **Connecticut**
2015 **Connecticut**
2014 **Connecticut**
2013 **Connecticut**
2012 **Baylor**
2011 **Texas A&M**
2010 **Connecticut**
2009 **Connecticut**
2008 **Tennessee**
2007 **Tennessee**
2006 **Maryland**

2005 **Baylor**
2004 **Connecticut**
2003 **Connecticut**
2002 **Connecticut**
2001 **Notre Dame**
2000 **Connecticut**
1999 **Purdue**
1998 **Tennessee**
1997 **Tennessee**
1996 **Tennessee**
1995 **Connecticut**
1994 **North Carolina**
1993 **Texas Tech**

1992 **Stanford**
1991 **Tennessee**
1990 **Stanford**
1989 **Tennessee**
1988 **Louisiana Tech**
1987 **Tennessee**
1986 **Texas**
1985 **Old Dominion**
1984 **USC**
1983 **USC**
1982 **Louisiana Tech**

NBA

WARRIORS KEEP FLYING HIGH!
Golden State's Andre Iguodala soars to the hoop as he helps the Warriors win their third NBA championship in four seasons. Once again, they had to battle the great LeBron James and the Cleveland Cavaliers . . . but once again, Golden State's depth was the difference.

What a Ride!

The 2017–18 NBA season proved one thing: **LeBron James** is the best player in the world . . . and the Golden State Warriors are the best TEAM in the world. In basketball, team beats player almost every time. For the third time in the past four seasons, that was true as the Warriors captured the NBA championship.

The regular season was packed with headlines way before the NBA Finals (page 105).

Before the season, NBA fans tracked lots of player moves. **Kyrie Irving** moved to the Boston Celtics, **Paul George** and **Carmelo Anthony** joined the Thunder, and **Dwyane Wade** went to Cleveland. Another big story was the rise of the Philadelphia 76ers. For several seasons, the team had lost . . . big time! The owners of the team called those bad seasons "The Process." They were slowly building their young team to be good. While they built, the 76ers lost and lost. In 2018, The Process paid off. Led by **Ben Simmons**, **Joel Embiid**, and **J. J. Redick**, the Sixers romped to the third-best record

in the East. They played a high-energy style that thrilled their fans. Philly entered the playoffs on a 16-game winning streak. Also in the East, the Boston Celtics burst out of the gate. At one point they reeled off a 16-game winning streak of their own to join the top ranks of the conference.

In the West, the big story was the Beard! That's the nickname for All-Everything **James Harden**. His Houston Rockets team added super point guard **Chris Paul** and the Rockets were flying! Harden poured in points, Paul dished, and rising star **Clint Capela** rocked the boards. The Rockets finished with the best record in the NBA, winning a team-record 65 games.

New Orleans had a rising superstar in **Anthony Davis** and looked headed for greatness until **DeMarcus Cousins** was lost to injury. The San Antonio Spurs put

Ben Simmons helped the Sixers reach the playoffs.

> **"It's not gonna happen overnight. The more you work, the more you figure out how to be great. Just keep adjusting, keep adapting."**
>
> —**JAMES HARDEN** ON HOW HE WORKS TO IMPROVE

James Harden had his eye on the ball . . . and the basket . . . and led the NBA in scoring.

together an NBA-best 21st straight winning season.

Minnesota made Timberwolves fans happy by earning the team's first playoff spot in 14 years. Fans also watched in awe as Oklahoma City's **Russell Westbrook** grabbed 20 rebounds in the season's final game. That was enough to make him the first player ever to average a triple-double for a season . . . twice! As great as Westbrook was, the Thunder didn't make it out of the first round of the playoffs.

Speaking of the playoffs, they proved what we said at the top: a great team will always beat a great player. The Warriors did just that and carried home the hardware.

2017–18 FINAL NBA STANDINGS

EASTERN CONFERENCE

ATLANTIC DIVISION

Raptors	59–23
Celtics	55–27
76ers	52–30
Knicks	29–53
Nets	28–54

CENTRAL DIVISION

Cavaliers	50–32
Pacers	48–34
Bucks	44–38
Pistons	39–43
Bulls	27–55

SOUTHEAST DIVISION

Heat	44–38
Wizards	43–39
Hornets	36–46
Magic	25–57
Hawks	24–58

WESTERN CONFERENCE

NORTHWEST DIVISION

Trail Blazers	49–33
Thunder	48–34
Jazz	48–34
Timberwolves	47–35
Nuggets	46–36

SOUTHWEST DIVISION

Rockets	65–17
Pelicans	48–34
Spurs	47–35
Mavericks	24–58
Grizzlies	22–60

PACIFIC DIVISION

Warriors	58–24
Clippers	42–40
Lakers	35–47
Kings	27–55
Suns	21–61

2018 NBA Playoffs

Lessons from the NBA Playoffs:

* Finishing with the best record in a conference did not translate to a spot in the NBA Finals.

* Having the best all-around guard in the league didn't mean you got out of the first round.

* **Anthony Davis** of the Pelicans is going to be a monster player very soon.

* Having **LeBron James** on your team is a great way to win.

First Round:
All the higher seeded teams in the East won their opening series. In the West, the New Orleans Pelicans and Utah Jazz were upset winners, showing off young talent like Davis and Utah's **Donovan Mitchell**.

Second Round:
With the top eight teams moving on, it was surprising to find four fairly easy wins in the second round. The Celtics' veterans showed the young Sixers they had more to learn. Cleveland swept top-seeded Toronto, with James averaging 34 points a game! Golden State rolled over New Orleans and Houston beat Utah.

Conference Finals:
Now we're talking! Both of these series went seven hard-fought games. When **Steph Curry** went a bit cold, **Kevin Durant** stepped up and led the Warriors. Not even the Beard could prevent Golden State from winning the last two games to clinch a spot in the Finals. In the East, James put the Cavs on his shoulders and carried them past a tough Celtics team. Like Golden State, Cleveland had to come from behind the final two games.

Mitchell (45) led the Jazz into the second round.

2018 NBA FINALS
Golden State...Again!

For the first time in NBA history, the same two teams met in the NBA Finals four years in a row. Golden State and Cleveland have become the biggest ongoing rivalry in sports. (Timeout! With **LeBron James** moving to the Lakers, it's over!) The Warriors' great team got even better in 2016 with the addition of **Kevin Durant**. In 2018, not even LeBron James was enough to overcome the team-wide excellence of the Warriors.

GAME 1: Warriors 124 Cavaliers 114
James did his best, pouring in a career playoff–high 51 points. Teammate **J. R. Smith** did not do his best. After grabbing a rebound of his own missed free throw with 4.5 seconds left, Smith chose to dribble backward instead of shooting. One problem: Cleveland was not ahead, the game was tied. If he had shot, the Cavs probably would have won. Instead, in overtime Golden State romped. After the series was over, James revealed that he had punched a blackboard

Durant rose up to win his second straight Final MVP.

in anger afterward and hurt his hand.

GAME 2: Warriors 122 Cavaliers 103
Steph Curry is probably the best three-point shooter in history. He added another page to his record book, making an all-time NBA single-game playoff best nine treys. His 33 points led the way as the Warriors won again.

GAME 3: Warriors 110 Cavaliers 102
As good as he was in Game 2, Curry was the opposite in Game 3. Fellow sharpshooter **Klay Thompson** was also off-target. No problem—Durant simply scored 43 and had 13 rebounds to dominate the game.

GAME 4: Warriors 108 Cavaliers 85
Curry was back on target and Golden State easily wrapped up its third NBA title in four seasons, including the past two in a row. He scored 37, including seven more three-pointers. It was a Golden State indeed!

NBA Awards

MOST VALUABLE PLAYER
JAMES HARDEN
ROCKETS

ROOKIE OF THE YEAR
BEN SIMMONS
76ERS

SIXTH MAN AWARD
LOU WILLIAMS
CLIPPERS

DEFENSIVE PLAYER OF THE YEAR
RUDY GOBERT
JAZZ

MOST IMPROVED PLAYER
◀◀◀ VICTOR OLADIPO
PACERS

SPORTSMANSHIP AWARD
KEMBA WALKER
HORNETS

COACH OF THE YEAR
DWANE CASEY
RAPTORS

LIFETIME ACHIEVEMENT AWARD
OSCAR ROBERTSON

59

Talk about a tough business! That is how many victories coach **Dwane Casey** led the Raptors—the most in the Eastern Conference. But a poor playoff run led to the Coach of the Year . . . being fired!

NBA Stat Leaders

30.4 POINTS PER GAME
James Harden, Rockets

10.2 ASSISTS PER GAME
Russell Westbrook, Thunder ▶▶▶

.468 3-POINT PCT.
Darren Collison, Pacers

2.57 BLOCKS PER GAME
Anthony Davis, Pelicans

16.0 REBOUNDS PER GAME
Andre Drummond, Pistons

.652 FIELD GOAL PCT.
Clint Capela, Rockets

2.36 STEALS PER GAME
Victor Oladipo, Pacers

2,251 **LeBron James** led the NBA with that many points. However, he played in 10 more games than Harden. NBA stats leaders are on a "per-game" average, not on season totals.

In the Paint

Fultz had his own triple-double at 19 years and 317 days!

◀◀◀ Superman in the House!

Veteran center **Dwight "Superman" Howard** has been scaring opponents since 2004. In March, he put together a game for the ages. He scored 32 points and pulled down an amazing 30 rebounds! It was only the second 30-30 game in the past 36 seasons!

Thanks, Kobe!

Los Angeles Lakers fans honored all-time great **Kobe Bryant** in a ceremony during a game in December. He led the Lakers to five championships and is third all-time in scoring in the NBA. Bryant changed jersey numbers during his career—from 8 to 24. So he became the first player to have two jersey numbers retired by a team!

Young Stars

Lonzo Ball came into the league with enormous hype, but injuries slowed his rookie season. Still, in a November game, he became the youngest player in NBA history to record a triple-double in a game. He was only 20 years and 15 days old when he did it against the Milwaukee Bucks. *Timeout!* Lonzo's record fell in April when Philadelphia's **Markelle**

Huge Night!

Houston's **James Harden** is no stranger to outstanding performances. In a January win over Orlando, he topped even himself. He scored 60 points and had 11 assists and 10 rebounds—a triple-double. It was the most

Pickup All-Stars

When you play with your pals, you pick teams, right? A couple of kids get to be captains and they take turns choosing players. In 2018, the NBA had a pickup All-Star Game. **LeBron James** and **Steph Curry** were the captains. They picked one by one from a list of All-Stars chosen by fans and coaches. It was a fun change to a game usually played East vs. West. All-Star Games are usually low-defense, high-scoring games and this was no different. The teams combined for 293 points! Team LeBron ended up on top, as James scored 29 and won the game's MVP trophy.

◀◀◀Super Sixth

In the NBA, the "sixth man" is a team's key sub. He's the first guy off the bench, a player who brings energy and action to a tired team. In 2017–18, the Clippers had one of the best ever. Guard **Lou Williams** became the first sixth man in NBA history to average 20 points and 5 assists off the bench. In a tough season for LA, Williams also was the Clippers' leader in points and assists per game. Maybe he should have been a starter!

Sweet Story

Though they improved by nine wins, the Lakers' season was over early. It ended nicely, though. For the final two games, the team called up guard **Andre Ingram** from the G League, an NBA minor league. Ingram was 32 and had been playing in the minors for ten seasons. He made the most of his chance, thrilling fans and even opponents with his outside shooting. In his first NBA game, he scored 19 points!

points ever scored by a player who hit double digits three times in a game. He was extra good from the free-throw line, making 17 of his 18 shots there.

Ouch!

Some nights, a team just wants to climb on the bus and forget what just happened. The Memphis Grizzlies had one of those games in March. Charlotte whomped them, 140–79. If you do the math, that's a 61-point difference. It was the first 60-point win (and first 60-point loss!) since 1998 and only the sixth such blowout in NBA history.

◀◀◀Scoring Streak

On January 5, 2007, **LeBron James** scored 8 points in a win by Cleveland over Milwaukee. Since then, he has never scored less than 10 points in a game. In March, he made it 867 double-digit games in a row, breaking an NBA record set by the great **Michael Jordan**. James finished the season on an 873-game 10-points-plus streak.

2017 WNBA

Allisha Gray led her team to the playoffs.

The 2017 season saw some top WNBA teams fade a bit, while others rejoined the championship hunt.

Indiana had made the playoffs for 12 straight years, but missed out in 2017. Losing star **Angel McCoughtrey** for a season was one reason Atlanta also ended its season without a postseason spot. Chicago's lone bright spot was a midseason 100–76 win over Eastern Conference champ Minnesota. The San Antonio Stars had high hopes, thanks to top draft pick **Kelsey Plum**, but her ankle injury limited her play until late in the season.

Meanwhile, the Dallas Wings made the playoffs for the first time since moving to Texas from Oklahoma in 2016. One big reason was the play of WNBA Rookie of the Year **Allisha Gray**. The Connecticut Sun earned its first playoff spot since 2012, even earning a first-round bye.

The top three teams remained the same, however, with the New York Liberty, Los Angeles Sparks, and Minnesota Lynx earning the highest regular-season spots.

Looking at the 2018 season, one team has a new home. The San Antonio Stars are moving to Las Vegas and will become the Aces. The Nevada city now has an NHL team, the Golden Knights, and will soon welcome the NFL's Raiders.

WNBA Playoffs

SEMIFINAL 1

The defending champion LA Sparks rolled over the Phoenix Mercury in the first two games of this series. It looked like an easy sweep in Game 3 before superstar **Diana**

2017 AWARDS WINNERS

MVP: Sylvia Fowles, Minnesota
ROOKIE OF THE YEAR: Allisha Gray, Dallas
DEFENSIVE PLAYER OF THE YEAR: Alana Beard, Los Angeles
MOST IMPROVED PLAYER: Jonquel Jones, Connecticut
SIXTH WOMAN: Sugar Rodgers, New York

Fowles and the Lynx pounded the Sparks.

off her shot and they held on for a hometown win. League MVP Fowles set a WNBA record with 17 rebounds in the game.

GAME 3: Sparks 75, Lynx 64
LA's strong defense prevented another tight finish. The Sparks' **Nneka Ogwumike** had a double-double with 16 points and 10 rebounds.

GAME 4: Lynx 80, Sparks 69
Minnesota forced a Game 5 on their home court with this big win in LA. It was a hard-fought game, with players hitting the court left and right. Fowles played almost blind for five minutes after being poked in the eye. But she managed a game-high 22 points to set up a rematch of the 2016 final game.

GAME 5: Lynx 85, Sparks 76
On their home court, Minnesota powered to its fourth WNBA title. That made them the second team ever with that many. Finals MVP Fowles led the way by breaking her own record with 20 rebounds. Though LA got to within three points in the final minute, Minnesota held on for the championship.

Taurasi made a series of late-game three-pointers. A last-play layup by **Candace Parker** gave LA the sweep and a return to the WNBA Finals.

SEMIFINAL 2
Having a pair of MVPs on your team sure makes winning easier! The Minnesota Lynx swept the Washington Mystics behind the shooting power of former MVP **Maya Moore** and new 2017 MVP **Sylvia Fowles**. That set up a rematch of the 2017 final series against the Sparks.

WNBA Finals

GAME 1: Sparks 85, Lynx 84
Minnesota's home crowd did their best, but their cheers could not polish off LA. The Lynx came back from 26 points behind. The Sparks had the last shot, though, and **Chelsea Gray** buried it for the win.

GAME 2: Lynx 70, Sparks 68
Another tight game . . . another fantastic finish. This time, though, the Lynx wouldn't let Gray get

2017 WNBA FINAL STANDINGS

EASTERN CONFERENCE		WESTERN CONFERENCE	
Liberty	22-12	**Lynx**	27-7
Sun	21-13	**Sparks**	26-8
Mystics	18-16	**Mercury**	18-16
Sky	12-22	**Wings**	16-18
Dream	12-22	**Storm**	15-19
Fever	9-25	**Stars**	8-26

NBA CHAMPIONS

2017–18 **Golden State**	2002–03 **San Antonio**	1987–88 **LA Lakers**
2016–17 **Golden State**	2001–02 **LA Lakers**	1986–87 **LA Lakers**
2015–16 **Cleveland**	2000–01 **LA Lakers**	1985–86 **Boston**
2014–15 **Golden State**	1999–00 **LA Lakers**	1984–85 **LA Lakers**
2013–14 **San Antonio**	1998–99 **San Antonio**	1983–84 **Boston**
2012–13 **Miami**	1997–98 **Chicago**	1982–83 **Philadelphia**
2011–12 **Miami**	1996–97 **Chicago**	1981–82 **LA Lakers**
2010–11 **Dallas**	1995–96 **Chicago**	1980–81 **Boston**
2009–10 **LA Lakers**	1994–95 **Houston**	1979–80 **LA Lakers**
2008–09 **LA Lakers**	1993–94 **Houston**	1978–79 **Seattle**
2007–08 **Boston**	1992–93 **Chicago**	1977–78 **Washington**
2006–07 **San Antonio**	1991–92 **Chicago**	1976–77 **Portland**
2005–06 **Miami**	1990–91 **Chicago**	1975–76 **Boston**
2004–05 **San Antonio**	1989–90 **Detroit**	1974–75 **Golden State**
2003–04 **Detroit**	1988–89 **Detroit**	1973–74 **Boston**

1972-73 **New York**	1954-55 **Syracuse**	1949-50 **Minneapolis**
1971-72 **LA Lakers**	1953-54 **Minneapolis**	1948-49 **Minneapolis**
1970-71 **Milwaukee**	1952-53 **Minneapolis**	1947-48 **Baltimore**
1969-70 **New York**	1951-52 **Minneapolis**	1946-47 **Philadelphia**
1968-69 **Boston**	1950-51 **Rochester**	
1967-68 **Boston**		
1966-67 **Philadelphia**		

WNBA CHAMPIONS

1965-66 **Boston**	2017 **Minnesota**	2006 **Detroit**
1964-65 **Boston**	2016 **Los Angeles**	2005 **Sacramento**
1963-64 **Boston**	2015 **Minnesota**	2004 **Seattle**
1962-63 **Boston**	2014 **Phoenix**	2003 **Detroit**
1961-62 **Boston**	2013 **Minnesota**	2002 **Los Angeles**
1960-61 **Boston**	2012 **Indiana**	2001 **Los Angeles**
1959-60 **Boston**	2011 **Minnesota**	2000 **Houston**
1958-59 **Boston**	2010 **Seattle**	1999 **Houston**
1957-58 **St. Louis**	2009 **Phoenix**	1998 **Houston**
1956-57 **Boston**	2008 **Detroit**	1997 **Houston**
1955-56 **Philadelphia**	2007 **Phoenix**	

A CAPITAL EVENT

The Washington Capitals won their first Stanley Cup. They had to overcome the surprise story of the season, the Las Vegas Golden Knights, who made it to the final in their first season in the league! Washington's win was extra-special for veteran captain Alex Ovechkin, an all-time star in his 13th season . . . and his first Stanley Cup!

Desert Hockey?

NHL 2017–18

The biggest story in hockey this season took place in the Mojave Desert, home of the Vegas Golden Knights. The team was formed through an expansion draft in June 2017. The Knights picked one unprotected player from each of the other 30 NHL teams. They ended up with a few well-known players, like **James Neal**, **David Perron**, and former Penguins goalie **Marc-Andre Fleury**. The rest of the team was mostly solid players who were not stars.

The city was excited to welcome hockey. In their first game, the Knights defeated the Arizona Coyotes 5–2, and there was no looking back. The fans loved the stadium's laser light shows, which had skating knights having sword fights before the games. After all . . . it was Vegas!

Meanwhile, Fleury, a backup goalie on his old team, seemed to be reborn. He delivered a record-breaking season. The expansion team from Las Vegas landed at the top of the Pacific Division with 51 wins. It was the first time an expansion team in any North American professional sport did so well in their first season.

MacKinnon had a solid season for Colorado.

Around the rest of the league, the winners and losers were changing. Former Eastern Conference powerhouses like the New York Rangers, Montreal Canadiens, Detroit Red Wings, and Chicago Blackhawks all missed the playoffs. In their place, some teams with mostly younger players were on the rise. For the New Jersey Devils, **Taylor Hall** delivered an incredible season. In the Western Conference, the Winnipeg Jets finished second, thrilling their dedicated fans.

However, the biggest surprise (other than Vegas) came out of Colorado. The Avalanche won just 22 games in the 2016–17 season, and many expected them to continue that poor record. With a lot of grit and an amazing season from center **Nathan MacKinnon**, they won 43 games, including a defeat of the St. Louis Blues on the last day of the season to claim a playoff spot.

Some regular contenders stayed firmly in their spots, too, with the Washington Capitals once again winning the Metropolitan Division, and the Pittsburgh Penguins making the playoffs for the 12th

Marc-Andre Fleury led the Knights to the Stanley Cup Final in the team's first season.

straight season. The Tampa Bay Lightning won the Atlantic Division on the strength of a huge season from **Nikita Kucherov** and their star, **Steven Stamkos**, remaining healthy. The Nashville Predators posted the best overall record of the regular season.

They were not led by a star, but by a deep group—*seven* of the team's forwards scored at least 35 points! Could they return to the Final? All in all, it was an exciting season featuring a lot of fresh faces, and a brand-new team that defied the odds.

2017–18 NHL FINAL STANDINGS

EASTERN CONFERENCE

ATLANTIC DIVISION

Tampa Bay	113
Boston	112
Toronto	105
Florida	96
Detroit	73
Montreal	71
Ottawa	67
Buffalo	62

METROPOLITAN DIVISION

Washington	105
Pittsburgh	100
Philadelphia	98
Columbus	97
New Jersey	97
Carolina	83
NY Islanders	80
NY Rangers	77

WESTERN CONFERENCE

CENTRAL DIVISION

Nashville	117
Winnipeg	114
Minnesota	101
Colorado	95
St. Louis	94
Dallas	92
Chicago	76

PACIFIC DIVISION

Vegas	109
Anaheim	101
San Jose	100
Los Angeles	98
Calgary	84
Edmonton	78
Vancouver	73
Arizona	70

NHL Playoffs

Nashville reached the conference final.

ROUND 2

→ The defending champion Pittsburgh Penguins faced the Washington Capitals for the third consecutive year and the 11th time in each team's playoff history (the Penguins won nine of those series). Washington's **Evgeny Kuznetsov** scored an exciting breakaway goal in overtime of Game 6 that won the series. The victory also sent Washington to their first Eastern Conference Final since 1998.

→ The series between the Nashville Predators and Winnipeg Jets raged on to Game 7, a winner-take-all showdown in Nashville. The Jets scored two goals in the first period, quieted the loud Predators crowd, and coasted to a 5-1 win.

ROUND 1

→ The Toronto Maple Leafs matched their lightning speed against the Boston Bruins' experience. Toronto took it to six games, but veteran Bruins forward **Patrice Bergeron** notched a goal and two assists in a Game 6 7–4 Boston win.

→ The Nashville Predators, the playoff team with the best regular-season record, faced off against the Colorado Avalanche, which had the worst record of any playoff team. It was a surprisingly close series. Colorado forced a Game 6 with a big win, but in the deciding contest, Predators goaltender **Pekka Rinne** sealed the series with a shutout.

ROUND 3

→ The star-studded series between Tampa Bay and Washington was a thriller. The Capitals piled on the scoring, winning the first two games, but the Lightning answered by taking the next two. The Lightning's forward **Ryan Callahan** had a goal and an assist in a Game 5 win, but Capitals goalie **Braden Holtby**'s Game 6 shutout led to a tense Game 7. Washington star **Alexander Ovechkin** scored a minute into the game. Teammate **André Burakovsky** scored two goals and Holtby had another shutout as the Capitals earned their second-ever trip to the Stanley Cup Final.

→ The playoff excitement grew with each series as fresh faces made their marks. In one of the most surprising matchups, the Vegas Golden Knights and the Winnipeg Jets both made their Conference Final debuts. It looked like the Knights' magic ride was ending when the Jets grabbed Game 1. But relentless pressure, the goal scoring of **Jonathan Marchessault** and **Reilly Smith**, plus the spectacular goaltending of **Marc-Andre-Fleury**, inspired the Knights to roll off four wins and a trip to the Stanley Cup Final.

2018 Stanley Cup Final

The drama was high when the Washington Capitals met the Vegas Golden Knights in the Stanley Cup Final. It was the first time since 2007 that neither of the two Final teams had ever won a Cup. In fact, the Knights were the first expansion team ever in any major North American sport to reach the final in their first season.

Game 1 in Las Vegas saw the lead change four times before the Knights' **Tomas Nosek** scored the game-winning goal. Game 2 was fast and hard. The Capitals' **Alexander Ovechkin** led the attack with big hits and snapped home the game-winning goal to even the series.

When the Capitals returned home, they turned up the heat. Ovechkin and **Evgeny Kuznetsov** scored goals and goalie **Braden Holtby** continued his fine play. The Capitals took a 2–1 edge in the series. Kuznetsov continued his dominance in Game 4 with four assists, as the Capitals crushed the Knights 6–2 and took a 3–1 series lead.

The series returned to Las Vegas for Game 5, and the Knights put up a heroic fight. Tied 1–1, Vegas's **Reilly Smith** punched home a goal to give the Golden Knights the lead. The Capitals stormed in the third period, with **Devante Smith-Pelly** diving to the ice to snap in the tying goal. Lars Eller poked home a loose puck for the game-winner. The Capitals won the game 4–3 and the Cup.

Alexander Ovechkin won the Conn Smythe Trophy as playoffs MVP.

Smith-Pelly's diving play led to a key goal.

On the Ice

NEW RULES: The rules of the game changed a bit for 2017–18. After an icing call, the team playing defense can't take a time out. When a team is called for icing, they can't change players until after the faceoff, so one strategy had been to give their tired players a rest by calling a time out. But that's no longer allowed. The other important rule change involves the coach's challenge of a goal scored after a team was offside. If a coach challenges an offside goal and loses the challenge, his team will get a delay of game penalty.

SUDDEN GOALIE:
Scott Foster is a 36-year-old accountant who plays in an amateur hockey league. His team's rink is near where the Chicago Blackhawks play. On March 29, 2018, the Blackhawks signed him to a one-day contract as their emergency backup goalie. Regular goalie **Corey Crawford** was injured and backup

Connor McDavid (97)

Anton Forsberg was hurt just before the game. Foster expected to sit in the locker room and watch the game on TV. But the third Blackhawks goalie, **Collin Delia**, left the game in the third period with leg cramps. So Foster actually had to play the last 14 minutes. He stopped all seven shots from the Winnipeg Jets and helped the Blackhawks win, 6–2. Surprised fans at the United Center chanted his name!

YOUNG STAR!: **Connor McDavid** won his second-straight Art Ross Trophy—given to the player who scores the most points in the regular season. The Edmonton Oilers center is just 21 years old. He became the youngest player to win back-to-back Ross trophies since **Wayne Gretzky**.

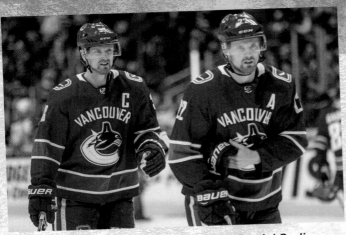

Identical superstars: Henrik and Daniel Sedin

TITANIC TWINS: When the season ended, **Daniel** and **Henrik Sedin**, brothers from Sweden who played 17 seasons for the Vancouver Canucks, decided to retire the same way they played— together. It marked the end of two remarkable careers that had been connected since the Canucks selected the identical twins No. 2 and No. 3 in the 1999 NHL draft. Henrik reached 1,000 points last season; Daniel did it this season. It's the first time two brothers reached 1,000 points each.

REAL GUTS: Just before the season opened, **Brian Boyle**, a 33-year-old forward for the New Jersey Devils, was diagnosed with chronic myeloid leukemia, a kind of cancer of the blood. He missed the first 10 games, but was on the ice in November and kept playing while also being treated. He ended the season with 69 games played, 13 goals, and 10 assists. Boyle also made his first appearance at the All-Star Game, replacing injured teammate **Taylor Hall**, where he got a huge ovation.

AWESOME OVI!: **Alexander Ovechkin** started his season with a roar, scoring two hat tricks and seven goals in his first two games of the season. He was the first player in 100 years to start the season with hat tricks in two straight games. The only other players to do that played in the very first season of the NHL—1917–18!

Keep That to Yourself

Feisty Boston Bruins forward **Brad Marchand** (right) inspired a new NHL rule during the playoffs. For some reason, Marchand licked the faces of opponents **Leo Komarov** of the Toronto Maple Leafs and **Ryan Callahan** of the Tampa Bay Lightning. He said it was to keep them from roughing him up. In the past, Marchand has kissed players, too, sometimes while fighting them! Kissing and licking were not against the rules–until now. The NHL told Marchand that if there was any more licking, he'd be called for a penalty!

2017-18 Awards

Hall was New Jersey's first Hart winner.

Calder Trophy
(Best Rookie)
MATHEW BARZAL, Islanders

Norris Trophy
(Best Defenseman)
VICTOR HEDMAN, Lightning

Selke Trophy
(Best Defensive Forward)
ANZE KOPITAR, Kings

Maurice Richard Trophy
(Top Goal Scorer)
ALEXANDER OVECHKIN, Capitals

Lady Byng Trophy
(Sportsmanship)
WILLIAM KARLSSON,
Golden Knights

Hart Trophy
(Most Valuable Player)
TAYLOR HALL, Devils

Ted Lindsay Award
(MVP as voted by players)
Art Ross Trophy
(Highest scorer)
CONNOR McDAVID, Oilers

Vezina Trophy
(Top Goaltender)
PEKKA RINNE, Predators

Masterton Trophy
(Dedication to Trophy)
BRIAN BOYLE, Devils

Jack Adams Award
(Coach of the Year)
GERARD GALLANT,
Golden Knights

Mark Messier Leadership Award
DERYK ENGELLAND,
Golden Knights

NHL Stat Champs

108 POINTS
Connor McDavid, Oilers

49 GOALS
Alexander Ovechkin, Capitals

2.09 GOALS AGAINST AVG.
.931 SAVE PCT.
Carter Hutton, Blues

68 ASSISTS
Claude Giroux, Flyers ▶▶▶

49 PLUS-MINUS
William Karlsson,
Golden Knights

44 GOALIE WINS
Connor Hellebuyck,
Jets

❝When G has the puck, it's just a matter of getting to the right spot because he's going to put it on your tape.❞
— **CLAUDE GIROUX'S** TEAMMATE TRAVIS KONECNY ON THE ACCURACY OF "G's" PASSES

Stanley Cup Champions

2017–18	Washington Capitals		1990–91	Pittsburgh Penguins
2016–17	Pittsburgh Penguins		1989–90	Edmonton Oilers
2015–16	Pittsburgh Penguins		1988–89	Calgary Flames
2014–15	Chicago Blackhawks		1987–88	Edmonton Oilers
2013–14	Los Angeles Kings		1986–87	Edmonton Oilers
2012–13	Chicago Blackhawks		1985–86	Montreal Canadiens
2011–12	Los Angeles Kings		1984–85	Edmonton Oilers
2010–11	Boston Bruins		1983–84	Edmonton Oilers
2009–10	Chicago Blackhawks		1982–83	New York Islanders
2008–09	Pittsburgh Penguins		1981–82	New York Islanders
2007–08	Detroit Red Wings		1980–81	New York Islanders
2006–07	Anaheim Ducks		1979–80	New York Islanders
2005–06	Carolina Hurricanes		1978–79	Montreal Canadiens
2004–05	No champion (Lockout)		1977–78	Montreal Canadiens
2003–04	Tampa Bay Lightning		1976–77	Montreal Canadiens
2002–03	New Jersey Devils		1975–76	Montreal Canadiens
2001–02	Detroit Red Wings		1974–75	Philadelphia Flyers
2000–01	Colorado Avalanche		1973–74	Philadelphia Flyers
1999–00	New Jersey Devils		1972–73	Montreal Canadiens
1998–99	Dallas Stars		1971–72	Boston Bruins
1997–98	Detroit Red Wings		1970–71	Montreal Canadiens
1996–97	Detroit Red Wings		1969–70	Boston Bruins
1995–96	Colorado Avalanche		1968–69	Montreal Canadiens
1994–95	New Jersey Devils		1967–68	Montreal Canadiens
1993–94	New York Rangers		1966–67	Toronto Maple Leafs
1992–93	Montreal Canadiens		1965–66	Montreal Canadiens
1991–92	Pittsburgh Penguins		1964–65	Montreal Canadiens

MOST STANLEY CUP TITLES

Montreal Canadiens 23
Toronto Maple Leafs 13
Detroit Red Wings 11
Boston Bruins 6
Chicago Blackhawks 6

1963–64	**Toronto Maple Leafs**
1962–63	**Toronto Maple Leafs**
1961–62	**Toronto Maple Leafs**
1960–61	**Chicago Blackhawks**
1959–60	**Montreal Canadiens**
1958–59	**Montreal Canadiens**
1957–58	**Montreal Canadiens**
1956–57	**Montreal Canadiens**
1955–56	**Montreal Canadiens**
1954–55	**Detroit Red Wings**
1953–54	**Detroit Red Wings**
1952–53	**Montreal Canadiens**
1951–52	**Detroit Red Wings**
1950–51	**Toronto Maple Leafs**
1949–50	**Detroit Red Wings**
1948–49	**Toronto Maple Leafs**
1947–48	**Toronto Maple Leafs**
1946–47	**Toronto Maple Leafs**
1945–46	**Montreal Canadiens**
1944–45	**Toronto Maple Leafs**
1943–44	**Montreal Canadiens**
1942–43	**Detroit Red Wings**
1941–42	**Toronto Maple Leafs**
1940–41	**Boston Bruins**
1939–40	**New York Rangers**
1938–39	**Boston Bruins**
1937–38	**Chicago Blackhawks**
1936–37	**Detroit Red Wings**
1935–36	**Detroit Red Wings**

1934–35	**Montreal Maroons**
1933–34	**Chicago Blackhawks**
1932–33	**New York Rangers**
1931–32	**Toronto Maple Leafs**
1930–31	**Montreal Canadiens**
1929–30	**Montreal Canadiens**
1928–29	**Boston Bruins**
1927–28	**New York Rangers**
1926–27	**Ottawa Senators**
1925–26	**Montreal Maroons**
1924–25	**Montreal Canadiens**
1923–24	**Montreal Canadiens**
1922–23	**Ottawa Senators**
1921–22	**Toronto St. Patricks**
1920–21	**Ottawa Senators**
1919–20	**Ottawa Senators**
1918–19	**Montreal Canadiens**
1917–18	**Toronto Arenas**

BACK WHERE IT BELONGS

The famous No. 3 car once belonged to the late great Dale Earnhardt, Sr. Now it's being driven by Austin Dillon. In the 2018 Daytona 500, No. 3 was No. 1 again as Dillon roared to his first victory in the sport's most famous race. Find out more about NASCAR, meet the 2017 champ, and more. Just turn the key, er . . . the page!

NASCAR

2017: A Monster Year!

NASCAR had a monster season in 2017, a Monster Energy season! That sports drink took over as the top sponsor of NASCAR's highest level of racing.

A new scoring system gave the drivers and crews monster headaches in the early going. Starting with 2017, each race was broken up into three stages. The driver in the lead after each of the first two stages earned extra points. The idea was to make the whole race an exciting one, not just the last few laps.

A handful of drivers won their first races at NASCAR's top level. In the No. 3 car, made famous by the great **Dale Earnhardt Sr., Austin Dillon** won in May in Charlotte for his first checkered flag. At Talladega, rising star **Ricky Stenhouse, Jr.,** also won his first career race. On his way to making the Chase for the Cup, **Ryan Blaney** captured the event in Pocono for his first win.

Bubba Wallace made history of another kind. He drove the No. 43 car in four races. He was just the second African American ever in NASCAR's top series, and it looks like he'll be a driver to watch in the coming seasons.

Jimmie Johnson, the defending champ, continued to cement his place in racing history. He won three races and moved into a tie for sixth place all-time with

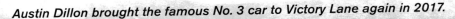

Austin Dillon brought the famous No. 3 car to Victory Lane again in 2017.

Good-bye, Junior, and thanks!

Rookie of the Year award, also just missed the Chase. He finished the season strong with 14 top-10 finishes, including five in the top 5.

Once the Chase for the Cup began, the action really heated up. Week by week, drivers moved into the next rounds or saw their championship hopes end. Finally, in Miami just before Thanksgiving, the final race was run and the 2017 champion emerged. Turn the page to follow the Chase and see who wound up on top!

83 victories. His career total has a long way to go to catch the all-time best total of 200 by **Richard Petty**.

Super-popular driver **Dale Earnhardt, Jr.,** retired at the end of the 2017 season, following a long good-bye tour for his millions of fans. **Carl Edwards**, a 28-time race winner, also took his final laps around the track. **Danica Patrick**, the first woman NASCAR driver, said she would drive one race in 2018 and then retire, too.

As for the Monster Energy championship, **Martin Truex Jr.,** was a man on a mission. He entered September leading in the points race with four race wins and 18 stage wins. **Kyle Busch** trailed him after winning two races. Those two race winners and 11 others were joined by non-winners **Matt Kenseth**, **Chase Elliott**, and **Jamie McMurray**. Perhaps the biggest surprise was young **Joey Logano**, who finished in the top four in 2016, but missed the playoffs in 2017. Even after finishing second in the final regular-season race at Richmond, Logano's points were not enough. **Erik Jones**, who won the

CHASE FOR THE CUP!

2017 FINAL STANDINGS

1. **Martin TRUEX, JR.**
2. **Kyle LARSON**
3. **Kyle BUSCH**
4. **Brad KESELOWSKI**
5. **Jimmie JOHNSON**
6. **Kevin HARVICK**
7. **Denny HAMLIN**
8. **Ricky STENHOUSE, JR.**
9. **Ryan BLANEY**
10. **Chase ELLIOTT**
11. **Ryan NEWMAN**
12. **Kurt BUSCH**
13. **Kasey KAHNE**
14. **Austin DILLON**
15. **Matt KENSETH**
16. **Jamie McMURRAY**

The Chase

A big win in Texas sent Kevin Harvick to the final race with a shot at the championship.

Challenger Round

CHICAGO: Martin Truex, Jr., the regular-season points leader, kept up his hot streak. He overcame a speeding penalty and loose lug nuts to capture this first playoff race and earned a spot in the next round.

NEW HAMPSHIRE: When you start from the pole, you've got a good shot at winning. That's what **Kyle Busch** did in this race. He moved on to the next round.

DOVER: Kyle Busch did it again, starting from the front and holding on for his second straight victory. Early success helped two drivers make it to the next round after earning points by winning the first stages.

OUT: Ryan Newman, Kurt Busch, Kasey Kahne, Austin Dillon

Contender Round

CHARLOTTE: Truex started way back in seventeenth place at the green flag in Charlotte. He battled through the pack all afternoon. At the end, he was in front for his sixth win in 2017.

TALLADEGA: A wild day at the track included several big crashes. Only 14 of the 43 cars that started finished the race! **Brad Keselowksi** won and earned his spot in the next round.

KANSAS: Truex kept his career-best season going with his seventh win of 2017. He also became the first driver ever to win six races on a 1.5-mile track in one season. Wrecks and blown engines sent four top drivers home from the Chase.

OUT: Matt Kenseth, Kyle Larson, Jamie McMurray, Ricky Stenhouse, Jr.

Eliminator Round

MARTINSVILLE: Kyle Busch won in overtime to clinch a spot in the Final Four in Miami. Several Chase drivers had a chance to win, but it was Busch who held on in a furious finish.

TEXAS: Kevin Harvick squeaked out the victory to clinch his spot in the Final Four. By finishing second, Truex also gained enough points to race for the title in Miami. That left only one spot remaining heading into Phoenix.

PHOENIX: Five drivers started with a chance at the one Final Four berth left. From that crowd, Keselowski came out ahead. He finished with enough points to become the fourth driver who could shoot for the Cup title in Miami. In this race, former champion **Matt Kenseth** won for possibly the final time, as he was expected to retire or cut way back on his driving in 2018.

OUT: Jimmie Johnson, Chase Elliott, Denny Hamlin, Ryan Blaney

Chase for the Cup Final

MIAMI: The driver who led just about every stats category in 2017 and who won the most races (eight) ended up where everyone thought he should—in first place in the last race. Martin Truex, Jr. won his first NASCAR championship by winning the final race of the season in Miami. He edged **Kurt Busch** after a furious finish. The two battled for the final dozen laps before Truex pulled away for the checkered flag and the biggest trophy of the year!

Truex won his first NASCAR title.

Other NASCAR Champs

Bell waved the championship flag after the final race.

Camping World Truck Series

With four wins, **Christopher Bell** won the regular-season points title and the top spot in the Camping World Truck Series playoffs. Seven other drivers made it into the seven-race, season-ending sprint to the trophy. Defending champion **Johnny Sauter** won a pair of playoff races, but Bell also won one. Bell then rolled to the season championship with a second-place finish in the final race in Miami. It was his final race in a truck, as he moved up to the Xfinity car series in 2018.

XFINITY SERIES

For the first time, the Xfinity Series championship was decided in a season-ending playoff series . . . just like in the larger Monster Energy series. Twelve drivers earned enough points to qualify for Xfinity's playoffs. (Monster drivers were not eligible.) **William Byron** won three races in the regular season to emerge as the points leader heading into the playoffs. Then he gave team owner **Dale Earnhardt, Jr.,** a great winning moment by earning the season points race after the final playoff race in Miami. "I don't think I breathed the last twenty laps," the 19-year-old driver said after picking up his trophy.

2017-18 NASCAR Highlights

Kevin Harvick (4) was out in front early and often in 2018.

Hot Starts!

Kevin Harvick got into the Final Four in 2017. In 2018, he charged out of the starting grid trying to make it back there. The driver they call "Happy" won three of the first four races of the season. They came in a row at Atlanta, Las Vegas, and Phoenix. He added two more wins before June. **Kyle Busch** was right on his heels. Busch also put together a triple-dip at Fort Worth, Bristol, and Richmond, adding a fourth early-season win later at Charlotte.

New for 2018

Like a busy mechanic, NASCAR is always under its own hood, looking for things to change.

❋ For 2018, new rules cut pit crew members from six to five. How would that affect drivers and pit stops?

❋ Fans saw a new car from the Chevrolet teams—the Camaro ZL1. Most NASCAR rides are based on four-door sedans. The Camaro is more like a high-powered sports car. **Austin Dillon** rode one to a Daytona 500 win (see box). Would the Camaro get more checkered flags?

❋ Where's Junior? **Dale Earnhardt, Jr.,** the most popular driver around, retired in 2017. Fans enjoyed seeing and hearing him in his new job as a TV analyst.

No. 3 Was No. 1 Again

The great **Dale Earnhardt, Sr.,** made the black No. 3 car a NASCAR legend. In 2018, **Austin Dillon** was in the famous car and drove it to victory in the season-opening Daytona 500. Earnhardt was well-known for his hard-charging style. He would have loved Dillon's win. The young driver smacked into rival **Aric Almirola** to take the lead late in the race. Then Dillon roared to the finish line ahead of nine other cars on the lead lap. It was the first Daytona win for Dillon.

NASCAR Champions

YEAR	DRIVER	CAR MAKER	YEAR	DRIVER	CAR MAKER
2017	Martin Truex, Jr.	Toyota	1995	Jeff Gordon	Chevrolet
2016	Jimmie Johnson	Chevrolet	1994	Dale Earnhardt, Sr.	Chevrolet
2015	Kyle Busch	Toyota	1993	Dale Earnhardt, Sr.	Chevrolet
2014	Kevin Harvick	Chevrolet	1992	Alan Kulwicki	Ford
2013	Jimmie Johnson	Chevrolet	1991	Dale Earnhardt, Sr.	Chevrolet
2012	Brad Keselowski	Dodge	1990	Dale Earnhardt, Sr.	Chevrolet
2011	Tony Stewart	Chevrolet	1989	Rusty Wallace	Pontiac
2010	Jimmie Johnson	Chevrolet	1988	Bill Elliott	Ford
2009	Jimmie Johnson	Chevrolet	1987	Dale Earnhardt, Sr.	Chevrolet
2008	Jimmie Johnson	Chevrolet	1986	Dale Earnhardt, Sr.	Chevrolet
2007	Jimmie Johnson	Chevrolet	1985	Darrell Waltrip	Chevrolet
2006	Jimmie Johnson	Chevrolet	1984	Terry Labonte	Chevrolet
2005	Tony Stewart	Chevrolet	1983	Bobby Allison	Buick
2004	Kurt Busch	Ford	1982	Darrell Waltrip	Buick
2003	Matt Kenseth	Ford	1981	Darrell Waltrip	Buick
2002	Tony Stewart	Pontiac	1980	Dale Earnhardt, Sr.	Chevrolet
2001	Jeff Gordon	Chevrolet	1979	Richard Petty	Chevrolet
2000	Bobby Labonte	Pontiac	1978	Cale Yarborough	Oldsmobile
1999	Dale Jarrett	Ford	1977	Cale Yarborough	Chevrolet
1998	Jeff Gordon	Chevrolet	1976	Cale Yarborough	Chevrolet
1997	Jeff Gordon	Chevrolet	1975	Richard Petty	Dodge
1996	Terry Labonte	Chevrolet	1974	Richard Petty	Dodge

YEAR	DRIVER	CAR MAKER	YEAR	DRIVER	CAR MAKER
1973	Benny Parsons	Chevrolet	1960	Rex White	Chevrolet
1972	Richard Petty	Plymouth	1959	Lee Petty	Plymouth
1971	Richard Petty	Plymouth	1958	Lee Petty	Oldsmobile
1970	Bobby Isaac	Dodge	1957	Buck Baker	Chevrolet
1969	David Pearson	Ford	1956	Buck Baker	Chrysler
1968	David Pearson	Ford	1955	Tim Flock	Chrysler
1967	Richard Petty	Plymouth	1954	Lee Petty	Chrysler
1966	David Pearson	Dodge	1953	Herb Thomas	Hudson
1965	Ned Jarrett	Ford	1952	Tim Flock	Hudson
1964	Richard Petty	Plymouth	1951	Herb Thomas	Hudson
1963	Joe Weatherly	Pontiac	1950	Bill Rexford	Oldsmobile
1962	Joe Weatherly	Pontiac	1949	Red Byron	Oldsmobile
1961	Ned Jarrett	Chevrolet			

2019 NASCAR HALL OF FAME CLASS

Davey Allison: Davey joins his father Bobby in the Hall of Fame, in part thanks to 19 career victories in nearly 200 career starts.

Jeff Gordon: One of NASCAR's most famous drivers, Jeff was third all-time with 93 race wins and second with four series championships. He made a record 797 starts in a row while helping expand NASCAR's fan base. He retired in 2016 and has become a popular NASCAR TV analyst.

Alan Kulwicki: One of the sport's rare owner/drivers, Alan had his best year in 1992, winning the season title.

Roger Penske: Better known for his 17 Indy 500 wins as a car owner, Penske also has a long record of success in NASCAR. His cars have won more than 100 races.

Jack Roush: Another all-star owner, Jack's cars and drivers have won more than 330 races all-time across all of NASCAR's divisions.

SHE PERSISTED!
Brittany Force steered this powerful Top Fuel dragster to the 2017 NHRA season championship. She was following in the tire tracks of her famous dad, John, who has won several championships. She was also the first woman to win Top Fuel in 35 years!

OTHER MOTOR SPORTS

2017 Formula 1

In 2017, **Lewis Hamilton** became the first British driver to win four career Formula 1 season championships. However, he had to battle another four-time winner to get it.

Germany's **Sebastian Vettel** won the title each year from 2010 to 2013. In 2017, he got the F1 season off to a roaring start with a victory in Australia. Vettel drives for Ferrari, and it was that carmaker's first win on the circuit since 2015. Then Mercedes, Hamilton's team, had won 19 out of 21 races in 2016. Was this the start of a new competition among the top carmakers?

Vettel won again in Bahrain three weeks later to move into first place. Ferrari has not been a champion car since 2007, so this early season success gave the company and its fans great hope for 2017.

Mercedes needed a win, which it got from an unusual source. Its No. 2 driver, **Valtteri Bottas** of Finland, held off Vettel to win in Russia for his first career victory. He won by only 0.6 seconds!

After clinching the title in his super-fast F1 car, Hamilton was lifted by his crew!

Vettel helped Ferrari nearly make it back to the top in 2017, but fell short of his fifth title.

Roaring from behind, though, was Hamilton, a fan favorite and former champion. He won a record fifth British Grand Prix in July to pull within one point of Vettel's season lead.

The two former champs continued to battle neck-and-neck. At Monza in Italy, Hamilton won, inching ahead by three points. It also made him the season's first back-to-back race winner. At the next race in Singapore, Vettel was in prime position to retake the series lead. He won the pole position on a track where passing is very difficult. But on the first lap, Vettel crashed! He was out of the race, and Hamilton roared to a third straight win. It moved the British driver 28 points in front of his rival heading into the season's final stretch of races.

Things got better for Hamilton and worse for Vettel after the race in Singapore. In Japan, Vettel had serious engine trouble early and only got in four laps. Hamilton kept his foot on the gas and won to increase his points lead. Then he won again in Texas at the United States Grand Prix, but could not shake Vettel, who stayed close with a second-place finish.

Finally, at the Mexican Grand Prix in late October, Hamilton earned enough points to clinch his fourth title. He finished ninth in the race, but he didn't care as he celebrated with fans. He became just the fourth driver ever with four F1 series wins.

2017 FORMULA 1 TOP DRIVERS

PLACE/DRIVER/TEAM	POINTS
1. Lewis **HAMILTON**, Mercedes	363
2. Sebastian **VETTEL**, Ferrari	317
3. Valtteri **BOTTAS**, Mercedes	305
4. Kimi **RÄIKKÖNEN**, Ferrari	205
5. Daniel **RICCIARDO**, Red Bull	200

Josef Newgarden was out in front for the season and showered with stars at the end.

2017 IndyCar

The tight turns of IndyCar racing led to a tight finish for the season championship. Heading into the final race, seven drivers had a shot at the title.

The high-speed action started early in 2017, as driver after driver took turns winning races. No one took command in the points race. Ten different drivers each won at least one event in the 17-race season. There were no two-time winners until **Graham Rahal** won the season's eighth race.

One of those 10 winners was Brazilian legend **Hélio Castroneves**. He's one of

the most successful drivers ever, but he had not won in more than three years. That changed in July, when he won at the Iowa Speedway. The victory brought him to 30 wins in his career.

The IndyCar race in Texas began with 22 drivers and ended with nine. A new design in the track turned it into a crash-filled spectacle. There were no major injuries, but several spectacular wrecks slowed down the race. **Will Power** wound up surviving, er . . . winning his second race of the year.

In racing, it's not how you start, but

2018 INDY 500
POWER UP!

Australian driver **Will Power** is an IndyCar veteran. He has won more than 19 races in the series, along with two dozen in other races around the world. Power had not landed the biggest prize . . . until he "powered" to victory in the 2018 Indy 500. In his eleventh try at winning at "The Brickyard," he roared to the lead late and held on tight! "I always wondered if I was going to win it," he said afterward. "I've had so many wins, and so many poles, but everybody always talked about the 500. It's just amazing. What an event. I love it." He also loved that the win pushed him into first place in the season series as he went after his second IndyCar title.

how you finish. American driver **Josef Newgarden** won three of five races heading into the season finale at Sonoma.

He took the series lead for the first time by winning at Mid-Ohio. That also made him the first driver to win three races in 2017. He added a fourth at Gateway Motorsports Park in Illinois and entered the final race weekend in prime position.

The season finale at the famous Sonoma, Calif., road course was worth double points, so six other drivers also entered the final weekend with a chance to win the title. Newgarden's closest challengers were Castroneves and two other former champs, **Scott Dixon** and **Simon Pagenaud**.

In an exciting race with several lead changes, Newgarden held them all off for the championship. His second-place finish behind Pagenaud gave him enough points to win his first career IndyCar season title. He was the first American to win since 2012 and

the first champion driver under the age of 30 since 2008.

The winner of that final race in Sonoma helped himself, too. Pagenaud, the 2016 series champ, moved from fourth to second overall for 2017.

INDYCAR 2017
FINAL STANDINGS

PLACE/DRIVER/COUNTRY	POINTS
1. **Josef Newgarden**, US	642
2. **Simon Pagenaud**, France	629
3. **Scott Dixon**, New Zealand	621
4. **Hélio Castroneves**, Brazil	598
5. **Will Power**, New Zealand	562
6. **Graham Rahal**, US	522
7. **Alexander Rossi**, US	494
8. **Takuma Sato**, Japan	441
9. **Ryan Hunter-Reay**, US	421
10. **Tony Kanaan**, Brazil	403

Drag Racing

TOP FUEL

Brittany Force became the first woman to win drag racing's top series in 35 years. She was just following in a family tradition. Her dad, **John Force**, has won numerous titles as a driver in Funny Car, and also as a team owner. Brittany used a late-season surge to get near the top on the final day of the season. At the last event in Pomona, Calif., she surged ahead in an early heat. That gave her enough points to clinch the season title over **Steve Torrence**.

FUNNY CAR

Robert Hight almost didn't get to enjoy his season title in this division for very long. After clinching the championship in an early round at Pomona, he kept racing. In the semifinal, his engine blew and his car fell apart in a fiery crash. Luckily, the champ was not injured.

PRO STOCK

This division had a nail-biting ending for the season title. In the final race of the year, **Bo Butner** edged **Tanner Gray** to win his first NHRA season championship title by only seven points over **Greg Anderson**.

PRO STOCK MOTORCYCLE

The motorcycle drag racing was much less of a nail-biter. **Eddie Krawiec** piled up his clinching points early in qualifying. It was the fourth series win for the two-wheel champ.

Robert Hight piloted this high-backed Funny Car to his second overall championship.

Motorcycle Racing

Gautier Paulin gets big air!

MOTOCROSS OF NATIONS

Motocross is the outdoor cousin of Supercross. It's very popular around Europe and riders have been churning dirt on tracks there for more than a century. Since 1947, the Motocross of Nations has matched the top riders in teams of three. In late 2017, the annual race was held in Great Britain. Though US riders have done well in the past, they finished well back in the pack this time. On top at the end was France. **Gautier Paulin**, **Romain Febvre**, and **Christophe Charlier** put together great runs and carried home the trophy. The Netherlands and "home team" Great Britain finished second and third.

SUPERCROSS

The dirt-churning, high-energy AMA Supercross 2018 season came down to the last race. **Jason Anderson** held a slim points lead over **Marvin Musquin**. How the two riders finished in the Las Vegas event would determine the overall champ. Musquin was among the leaders while Anderson hung back, determined to finish and clinch his title. When the checkered flag dropped, Musquin was second, but Anderson was fifth. That finish gave him a nine-point lead and his first Supercross championship. It was also the first title for his bike maker, Husqvarna Factory.

Jason Anderson cuts into a tight turn.

Major Champions
OF THE 2000s

TOP FUEL DRAGSTERS

YEAR	DRIVER
2017	Brittany Force
2016	Antron Brown
2015	Antron Brown
2014	Tony Schumacher
2013	Shawn Langdon
2012	Antron Brown
2011	Del Worsham
2010	Larry Dixon
2009	Tony Schumacher
2008	Tony Schumacher
2007	Tony Schumacher
2006	Tony Schumacher
2005	Tony Schumacher
2004	Tony Schumacher
2003	Larry Dixon
2002	Larry Dixon
2001	Kenny Bernstein

FUNNY CARS

YEAR	DRIVER
2017	Robert Hight
2016	Ron Capps
2015	Del Worsham
2014	Matt Hagan
2013	John Force
2012	Jack Beckman
2011	Matt Hagan
2010	John Force
2009	Robert Hight
2008	Cruz Pedregon
2007	Tony Pedregon
2006	John Force
2005	Gary Scelzi
2004	John Force
2003	Tony Pedregon
2002	John Force
2001	John Force

PRO STOCK CARS

YEAR	DRIVER
2017	Bo Butner
2016	Jason Line
2015	Erica Enders-Stevens
2014	Erica Enders-Stevens
2013	Jeg Coughlin, Jr.
2012	Allen Johnson
2011	Jason Line
2010	Greg Anderson
2009	Mike Edwards
2008	Jeg Coughlin, Jr.
2007	Jeg Coughlin, Jr.
2006	Jason Line
2005	Greg Anderson
2004	Greg Anderson
2003	Greg Anderson
2002	Jeg Coughlin, Jr.
2001	Warren Johnson

FORMULA 1

YEAR	DRIVER
2017	Lewis Hamilton
2016	Nico Rosberg
2015	Lewis Hamilton
2014	Lewis Hamilton
2013	Sebastian Vettel
2012	Sebastian Vettel
2011	Sebastian Vettel
2010	Sebastian Vettel
2009	Jenson Button
2008	Lewis Hamilton
2007	Kimi Räikkönen
2006	Fernando Alonso
2005	Fernando Alonso
2004	Michael Schumacher
2003	Michael Schumacher
2002	Michael Schumacher
2001	Michael Schumacher

INDYCAR SERIES

YEAR	DRIVER
2017	Josef Newgarden
2016	Simon Pagenaud
2015	Scott Dixon
2014	Will Power
2013	Scott Dixon
2012	Ryan Hunter-Reay
2011	Dario Franchitti
2010	Dario Franchitti
2009	Dario Franchitti
2008	Scott Dixon
2007	Dario Franchitti
2006	Sam Hornish, Jr.
2005	Dan Wheldon
2004	Tony Kanaan
2003	Scott Dixon
2002	Sam Hornish, Jr.
2001	Sam Hornish, Jr.

AMA SUPERCROSS

YEAR	DRIVER
2018	Jason Anderson
2017	Ryan Dungey
2016	Ryan Dungey
2015	Ryan Dungey
2014	Ryan Villopoto
2013	Ryan Villopoto
2012	Ryan Villopoto
2011	Ryan Villopoto
2010	Ryan Dungey
2009	James Stewart, Jr.
2008	Chad Reed
2007	James Stewart, Jr.
2006	Ricky Carmichael
2005	Ricky Carmichael
2004	Chad Reed
2003	Ricky Carmichael
2002	Ricky Carmichael
2001	Ricky Carmichael

AMA MOTOCROSS

YEAR	RIDER (MOTOCROSS)	RIDER (LITES)
2018		
2017	Eli Tomac	Zach Osborne
2016	Ken Roczen	Cooper Webb
2015	Ryan Dungey	Jeremy Martin
2014	Ken Roczen	Jeremy Martin
2013	Ryan Villopoto	Eli Tomac
2012	Ryan Dungey	Blake Baggett
2011	Ryan Villopoto	Dean Wilson
2010	Ryan Dungey	Trey Canard
2009	Chad Reed	Ryan Dungey
2008	James Stewart, Jr.	Ryan Villopoto
2007	Grant Langston	Ryan Villopoto
2006	Ricky Carmichael	Ryan Villopoto
2005	Ricky Carmichael	Ivan Tedesco
2004	Ricky Carmichael	James Stewart, Jr.
2003	Ricky Carmichael	Grant Langston
2002	Ricky Carmichael	James Stewart, Jr.
2001	Ricky Carmichael	Mike Brown

ACTION SPORTS

HIGH-FLYING RIDER!
Daredevil rider Travis Pastrana flew through the red, white, and blue smoke over 16 school buses. This was just one of three jumps he did live on TV to repeat a feat attempted by famous motorcycle man Evel Knievel. Did Pastrana land safely? See page 153 to find out.

Summer X Games

The Summer X Games were held in Minneapolis for the first time in 2017. A region covered in snow and ice for much of the year might not seem like a natural for summer action sports. Still, it was a big hit with fans and athletes. The success of the first X Games in Minneapolis meant a return trip in 2018.

▲Unplugged

To win gold in Women's Skateboard Street, **Mariah Duran** first got unplugged. "I take an hour at the beginning of every day, just for myself," she says. "I put the phone away and think about where I'm at and where I could be." Duran's daily meditation sessions paid off in her first X Games gold medal in 2018. She edged 16-year-old **Aori Nishimura**, the 2017 champ, by 1.66 points.

Fourth Time Is the Charm

Mitchie Brusco was just 16 when he landed the first 1080 in Skateboard Big Air at the X Games in Barcelona in 2013. Even still, X Games legend **Bob Burnquist** edged him out for the gold medal that year. In 2018, Brusco brought back the 1080 to the delight of the U.S. Bank Stadium crowd and the national TV audience. Three times, he tried to pull off the maneuver. Finally, on the fourth effort, he did it! And this time, it was good enough for gold.

Backup Bike

No bike? No problem! **Brandon Loupos'** bike was stolen shortly before the X Games. A backup bike arrived just in time for the start of his practice runs for BMX Dirt in Minneapolis. Maybe it took a little getting used to, because Loupos entered his final run in fourth place. Then on that run, the Australian went with a cash roll, triple tail whip, and flare double tail whip to stoke the crowd and wow the judges. Loupos'

2018 SUMMER X GAMES CHAMPS

BMX BIG AIR	James Foster	MOTO X QUARTERPIPE HIGH AIR	Axell Hodges
BMX DIRT	Brandon Loupos	MOTO X STEP UP	Jarryd McNeil
BMX PARK	Logan Martin	NEXT X SKATEBOARD PARK	Liam Pace
BMX PARK BEST TRICK	Alex Hiam	NEXT X SKATEBOARD STREET	Giovanni Vianna
BMX STREET	Chad Kerley	SKATEBOARD BIG AIR	Mitchie Brusco
BMX VERT	Vince Byron	M SKATEBOARD PARK	Alex Sorgente
HARLEY-DAVIDSON FLAT TRACK	Jared Mees	W SKATEBOARD PARK	Brighton Zeuner
HARLEY HOOLIGAN RACING	Daniel Mischler	M SKATEBOARD STREET	Nyjah Huston
MOTO X BEST TRICK	Jackson Strong	W SKATEBOARD STREET	Mariah Duran
MOTO X BEST WHIP	Jarryd McNeil	SKATEBOARD VERT	Jimmy Wilkins
MOTO X FREESTYLE	Tom Pagès		

95 points vaulted him past his fellow bikers for the gold medal. He knocked **Colton Walker**, the defending champion and a fan favorite who grew up in Minneapolis, off the podium to fourth place.

Summer X Notes

✱ At 14, **Brighton Zeuner** is already a two-time X Games champ. She defended her 2017 gold medal by winning Women's Skateboard Park.

✱ **Jackson Strong** won his fourth gold medal in Moto X Best Trick with one of Minnesota's favorite athletes cheering him on: **Harrison Smith**, the Minnesota Vikings' star safety. Smith has been an action sports fan since learning to ride dirt bikes when he was five.

✱ **Tom Pagès** go-for-broke Moto X Freestyle "style" is all-or-nothing. This year, it was all: He won his second gold medal in the event.

Vince Byron defended his BMX Vert gold.

Winter X Games

As sure as snow, winter in Colorado means the X Games in Aspen. In January 2018, the resort town hosted the Games for the 17th consecutive year. The world's best (and coldest!) action sports athletes didn't disappoint. Here are just a few of the highlights.

Teen Sensation

Chloe Kim tuned up for her historic performance at the 2018 Winter Olympic Games in Pyeongchang by winning the Women's Snowboard SuperPipe in Aspen. But it wasn't easy. The California teenager entered her final run in the unfamiliar position of needing to come from behind to win. Then she threw down back-to-back 1080s and edged Arielle Gold for the victory. Though Kim was still only 17 years old at the time (she turned 18 in the spring of 2018), it already was her third win in the event in Aspen.

Chloe Kim tuned up for the Olympics in Aspen.

What's Old Is New

The newest event at X Games Aspen was won by the oldest competitor. Forty-eight-year-old Travis Whitlock sped ahead of Logan Cipala—at 22, he was less than half Whitlock's age—to win the first gold medal in Snow Hill Climb. In Snow Hill Climb, riders race motorcycles up the flat bottom of the SuperPipe course. The bikes are modified with studs and screws in the tires to grip the ice so riders can go down . . . er, up! . . . the track. Competition is head-to-head, with the riders lining up next to each other at the base of the SuperPipe. Whitlock beat Cipala in the final by getting off the mark quickly, then strategically hugging the smoother side of the pipe to cruise to the win.

Change Can Be Good

Austrian Anna Gasser was forced to step out of her comfort zone in Aspen, and the result was golden. Not long before the Big Air event, organizers announced that the competitors would be required to do one trick spinning in each direction. "That was actually really hard for me," Gasser said. "With this change, I didn't think my chances were that good anymore."

Turcotte flew high above the snow to nail this trick.

Road Trip!

It's a pretty sure thing that no one was rooting more for **Brett Turcotte** to win a snowmobiling gold medal than his kids. And it's not just that they're, well, his kids… it's that he promised them a trip to Disneyland if he won! Turcotte not only won Snowmobile Speed & Style, but he followed that up with gold in Snowmobile Freestyle. Does that mean two trips to Disneyland?

But it also made her try things she never had in competition before. She responded to the challenge with an impressive Cab double 10. Then a textbook front double underflip gave her a solid lead, and she went on to win her first X Games gold medal.

"Four is my lucky number, I guess."

—**DAVID WISE**, AFTER WINNING CAREER GOLD MEDAL NO. 4 IN THE SKI SUPERPIPE WHILE POSTING THE FIRST RUN EVER TO FEATURE FOUR DOUBLE CORKS SPUN IN ALL FOUR DIRECTIONS.

2018 WINTER X GAMES CHAMPS

M SKI BIG AIR	**Henrik Harlaut**
W SKI BIG AIR	**Sarah Hoefflin**
M SKI SLOPESTYLE	**Henrik Harlaut**
W SKI SLOPESTYLE	**Maggie Voisin**
M SKI SUPERPIPE	**David Wise**
W SKI SUPERPIPE	**Maddie Bowman**
SNOW BIKE BEST TRICK	**Rob Adelberg**
SNOW BIKECROSS	**Cody Matechuk**
M SNOWBOARD BIG AIR	**Max Parrot**
W SNOWBOARD BIG AIR	**Anna Gasser**
M SNOWBOARD SLOPESTYLE	**Marcus Kleveland**
W SNOWBOARD SLOPESTYLE	**Jamie Anderson**
M SNOWBOARD SUPERPIPE	**Ayumu Hirano**
W SNOWBOARD SUPERPIPE	**Chloe Kim**
SNOW HILL CLIMB	**Travis Whitlock**
SNOWMOBILE FREESTYLE	**Brett Turcotte**
SNOWMOBILE SPEED & STYLE	**Brett Turcotte**
SPECIAL OLYMPICS UNIFIED SNOWBOARD	**Henry Meece-Chris Klug**

Lakey Peterson shoots the curl on her way to a win.

Action Notes

Mountain Running

For athletes who think cross country running isn't enough of a challenge and hiking isn't enough of a workout, there's mountain running. It combines the best of both those worlds in a grueling sport that is rapidly climbing in popularity (climbing . . . get it?).

Sometimes mountain runners run. Sometimes they hike. The trick is knowing when to do which on very different types of courses. In 2018, the National Mountain Running championships were held during the summer at Loon Mountain in Lincoln, New Hampshire. The top four finishers in both the men's and women's competition qualified for the US Mountain Running Team that competed in the World Championships in Andorra, in September.

World Surf League

Hawaii's **John John Florence** won the men's World Surf League championship for 2017. No surprise there! Florence established himself as the best in world en route to his first title in 2016 and didn't let up in '17. In 2018, though, Florence got off to a very slow start. *Big* surprise there! That made it anybody's tour to win. Sure enough, the first five events produced four different winners. Early in the summer, eighth-year pro **Julian Wilson** of Australia had the edge in a close race. On the women's side, Australian **Tyler Wright** won only one of the 10 events on tour in 2017. Her eight top-five finishes were enough to edge fellow countrywomen **Stephanie Gilmore** and **Sally Fitzgibbons** for her second title in a row. In 2018, Lakey Peterson of Santa Barbara, California, held a narrow lead over Gilmore at the halfway point of the season.

Storybook Ending ... Almost!

Surfing star Mick Fanning decided his heart wasn't all in for the rigors of competition anymore. So he decided he would retire following the World Surf League event early in 2018 at Bells Beach in his native Australia. It looked as if Fanning might go out with a victory—and windup his career as the world-ranked No. 1—but that magical finish was not meant to be. Brazilian Italo Ferreira moved ahead on his last wave, and Fanning settled for second place. Still, the three-time world champ had no regrets. "It has been an amazing career," Fanning said afterward. "I want to thank everyone along the way. I walk away with so many great memories."

Young at Heart

Known for its calm waters and great views, Italy's Lake Como is a picture of peace and quiet. But Italian racer Fabio Buzzi wasn't there in March 2018 for sightseeing. Instead, he was about to churn the waters of the peaceful lake with a noise-making attempt at a world diesel powerboat record. Buzzi, 75, climbed into his red hydroplane, and let 'er rip. He ended with a new world record speed of 277.515 kilometers per hour (172.44 miles per hour).

From One Legend to Another

Remember Travis Pastrana? The action sports legend was an X Games hero and race car driver. He continues to be the ringleader of Nitro Circus, an action sports franchise that includes a reality TV show, DVDs, and live events. In the summer of 2018, Pastrana pulled off what may be his most daring stunts yet. He re-created the motorcycle jumps of Evel Knievel. (Knievel was the original extreme sports star. In the 1960s and 1970s, he became known for his daredevil jumps and spectacular crashes while jumping his bike over cars.) In a live TV show, Pastrana successfully matched three of Knievel's most famous jumps. He flew over 52 cars, then over 16 buses, then over the huge fountain at Caesar's Palace in Las Vegas. Take that, Evel!

Pastrana celebrates a jump with a wheelie.

GOLF

WATCH WHAT HE DID!
As Brooks Koepka charged toward his second straight US Open win, a former pro was working as a TV announcer following Koepka's group. That announcer was Curtis Strange . . . who was the last golfer to go back-to-back at the Open!

Major Moments

The biggest story in men's golf in 2018 was the return of **Tiger Woods** to regular appearances. The megastar has been battling injuries and even had back surgery in 2017. But he kept working and practicing. By the time of the 2018 Masters, he was part of every weekend's "who is going to win" talk. He didn't win (but around the same time he was within a stroke of the lead at another tournament), but just having him at tournaments brought golf a lot of headlines.

Patrick Reed supplied the biggest headline at the Masters. Known more as a grinder than a smooth swinger like No. 1 player **Dustin Johnson** or playing partner **Rory McIlroy**, Reed did what it took to win. Being the underdog helped. Hearing louder cheers for other golfers, Reed said, "fueled my fire a little bit."

Reed led at the start of the final day, but had to watch his back. Former Masters champ **Jordan Spieth** made a charge, making up nine strokes. Reed stayed calm and put up four pars to wrap up his first major championship.

At the US Open, **Brooks Koepka** made it two in a row. The 2017 champ powered to his second win in the huge event. He was the first player since **Curtis Strange** way back in 1989 to go back-to-back. On a very tough course, he held off Johnson to win at one over par.

The British Open gave Woods fans a quick peek at his possible future. He began play on Sunday just a few strokes off the lead. A windy day kept scores high, however. Tiger finished three strokes behind. The winner became the first Italian player to capture the fabled British Open title.

MEN'S GRAND SLAM EVENTS

MASTERS	**Patrick Reed**
US OPEN	**Brooks Koepka**
BRITISH OPEN	**Francesco Molinari**
PGA CHAMPIONSHIP	**Brooks Koepka**

Francesco Molinari made birdie on the final hole to nail down his historic victory.

There were some good stories away from the majors. At the Arnold Palmer, McIlroy put on a great display of golf. He had birdies at five of the final six holes. He closed with a 31 on the back nine for a 64 on the day to win by three strokes.

At the WGC Mexico event, **Justin Thomas** was behind by 11 strokes after the first two rounds. His event was pretty much over . . . but no one told him that! Thomas shot a course record 62 in the third round. He came to the 18th hole on Sunday one shot from the lead. He landed an eagle from almost 120 yards out to tie with **Phil Mickelson**! Mickelson won in the playoff for his first win in five years, but Thomas's comeback was an equally big story.

Tiger Woods

2017 Presidents Cup

Every other year, the top US golfers tee off in a three-day event against golfers from around the world . . . except from Europe. The 2018 Presidents Cup, held in New Jersey, showed that the US still has an edge on its opponents. The Americans won for the tenth time in 12 tournaments, and seventh time in a row.

The event has four parts. Players team up to take part in foursomes or four-ball events. The winning teams get one point for a win and each team gets a half-point for a tie. After Thursday, the US led by two points. On Friday, they extended their lead by winning 4.5 of a possible five points. The US did even better Saturday, combining to score 6.5 points to the international team's 1.5 in eight matches.

The US team was so far ahead that they only needed two points from Sunday's 12 singles matches to clinch the cup.

Daniel Berger beat **Si Woo Kim** to get the points to snag the trophy.

Dustin Johnson had the most success, winning four of his matches and tying a fifth. **Justin Thomas** earned 3.5 points. **Jordan Spieth** and **Patrick Reed** played as a team four times and won three of their matches.

The success of the US team at this international golf event gave hope to Ryder Cup fans. That event, set for late 2018, matches US golfers against Europeans. They will give the Americans a much tougher battle than the Presidents Cup opponents.

Daniel Berger

THE US PRESIDENTS CUP TEAM

Daniel Berger	Dustin Johnson	Phil Mickelson
Kevin Chappell	Kevin Kisner	Patrick Reed
Rickie Fowler	Brooks Koepka	Jordan Spieth
Charley Hoffman	Matt Kuchar	Justin Thomas

LPGA 2018

The 2018 LPGA season featured some old faces coming back and some new stars rising up.

Michelle Wie won the 2018 HSBC Women's World Championship, played at a course in Singapore. Wie, 28, was a teenage sensation, but that was more than a decade ago. She has played well at times, but has had several injuries. She was also expected to be a megastar and that hasn't happened. She could have quit, but she kept playing. The win in Singapore was her first in four years. "I always think the best is in front of me," said Wie. "That's why I practice and work so hard."

Sung Hyun Park was the big story of the 2017 LPGA season. She won the US Women's Open and later became the No. 1 ranked player in the world. She was the first since **Nancy Lopez** in 1978 to be Player AND Rookie of the Year for the LPGA (she was co-player of the year with **So Yeon Ryu**). In 2018, Park continued her great play. At the Texas Classic, she buried a 20-yard chip to win the tournament. In July, she beat Ryu in a playoff to win her second major, the Women's PGA Championship. Can she repeat as Player of the Year in 2018?

Giving her a run will be **Ariya Jutanugarn**, who led the LPGA money list by more than $700,000 at one point, thanks to two big tournament wins including the US Open. The top rookie for most of the season was **Jin Young Ko**, who made the cut in her first nine tournaments. And watch for veteran **Sei Young Kim**. At the Thornberry Creek Classic, she finished at a new LPGA-record 31 under par.

Ariya Jutanugarn broke out for a great 2018.

WOMEN'S GRAND SLAM EVENTS

US WOMEN'S OPEN	**Ariya Jutanugarn**
WOMEN'S PGA	**Sung Hyun Park**
ANA INSPIRATION	**Pernilla Lindberg**
WOMEN'S BRITISH OPEN	**Georgia Hall**
THE EVIAN CHAMPIONSHIP	_____

Chip Shots

Finau almost created a Masters lowlight.

That's a Looonnnng Hole!

Early in 2018, **Adam Rolston** started playing on a golf hole. Almost three months later, he was still playing it! Rolston created a single "hole" across more than 1,200 miles of Mongolian countryside and towns. Shot by shot, he moved his ball across the fields and forests. He slept in a tent at night then got up and started swinging. He made more than 14,000 shots, the final one a putt on an actual golf green.

Quick Comeback

Tony Finau might have been a feel-bad story . . . but he turned into a feel-good one. On Wednesday of Masters week, he shot a hole-in-one in the Par 3 contest. He was so excited he started jumping up and down, until he landed

Not a Good Record to Have

Dustin Johnson was having a great 2017 . . . until he played in the HSBC Champions in Shanghai. He blew a record-setting six-shot lead and watched **Justin Rose** pass him for the win. Don't feel too sorry for Dustin, though—he made more than $8 million for the year!

27.88

Some people think golf is slow. **Tom Lovelady, Lanto Griffin, Andrew Yun,** and **Stephan Jaeger** beg to differ. The four PGA rookies set a new world record by playing a golf hole in Palm Springs in 27.88 seconds.

FUTURE STARS

Rookie players are always good to watch. After all, they are the stars of tomorrow. Some PGA rookies didn't let being young stop them from winning. In the first half of 2018, three first-year players captured tournament titles. **Austin Cook** won the RSM Classic in Georgia in late 2017. In April 2018, Japanese golfer **Satoshi Kodaira** *(left)* put on the winner's plaid jacket at the Heritage Classic in South Carolina. In May 2018, **Aaron Wise** not only won the Byron Nelson Classic, but he broke the tournament scoring record. His 23 under par was a new low by three strokes!

wrong and dislocated his ankle! Fans were amazed when he showed up Thursday to play— and shot a 68! He wound up tied for tenth place. Not bad for a guy with one good ankle!

Records Good and Bad

The good: At the TPC Deere Run event, **Michael Kim** earned his first victory— and then some! Kim won by eight strokes at 257 to set a new tournament record. The bad: **Sergio Garcia** scored a 13 on the 15th hole of the 2018 Masters. That is, believe it or not, an octuple-bogey! His biggest problem? Hitting three shots into the water . . . in a row!

Kim joined the ranks of top young golfers with his record score.

The Majors

In golf, some tournaments are known as the majors. They're the most important events of the year on the men's and women's pro tours. (There are four men's majors and five women's majors.) Among the men, **Jack Nicklaus** holds the record for the most all-time wins in the majors. **Patty Berg** won more majors than any other women's player.

MEN'S

	MASTERS	US OPEN	BRITISH OPEN	PGA CHAMP.	TOTAL
Jack **NICKLAUS**	6	4	3	5	**18**
Tiger **WOODS**	4	3	3	4	**14**
Walter **HAGEN**	0	2	4	5	**11**
Ben **HOGAN**	2	4	1	2	**9**
Gary **PLAYER**	3	1	3	2	**9**
Tom **WATSON**	2	1	5	0	**8**
Bobby **JONES**	0	4	3	0	**7**
Arnold **PALMER**	4	1	2	0	**7**
Gene **SARAZEN**	1	2	1	3	**7**
Sam **SNEAD**	3	0	1	3	**7**
Harry **VARDON**	0	1	6	0	**7**

RYDER CUP RESULTS

Note: The current format of the United States versus Europe began in 1979.

YEAR	WINNING TEAM	SCORE	YEAR	WINNING TEAM	SCORE
2018	_____	_____	1997	**EUROPE**	14.5–13.5
2016	**UNITED STATES**	17–11	1995	**EUROPE**	14.5–13.5
2014	**EUROPE**	16.5–11.5	1993	**UNITED STATES**	15–13
2012	**EUROPE**	14.5–13.5	1991	**UNITED STATES**	14.5–13.5
2010	**EUROPE**	14.5–13.5	1989	**TIE**	14–14
2008	**UNITED STATES**	16.5–11.5	1987	**EUROPE**	15–13
2006	**EUROPE**	18.5–9.5	1985	**EUROPE**	16.5–11.5
2004	**EUROPE**	18.5–9.5	1983	**UNITED STATES**	14.5–13.5
2002	**EUROPE**	15.5–12.5	1981	**UNITED STATES**	18.5–9.5
1999	**UNITED STATES**	14.5–13.5	1979	**UNITED STATES**	17–11

WOMEN'S

	LPGA	USO	BO	ANA	EV	MAUR	TH	WES	TOTAL
Patty **BERG**	0	1	0	0	0	0	7	7	15
Mickey **WRIGHT**	4	4	0	0	0	0	2	3	13
Louise **SUGGS**	1	2	0	0	0	0	4	4	11
Annika **SÖRENSTAM**	3	3	1	3	0	0	0	0	10
Babe **ZAHARIAS**	0	3	0	0	0	0	3	4	10
Betsy **RAWLS**	2	4	0	0	0	0	0	2	8
Juli **INKSTER**	2	2	0	2	0	1	0	0	7
Inbee **PARK**	3	2	1	1	0	0	0	0	7
Karrie **WEBB**	1	2	1	2	0	1	0	0	7

KEY: LPGA = LPGA Championship, USO = US Open, BO = British Open, ANA = ANA Inspiration, EV = Evian Championship, MAUR = du Maurier (1979–2000), TH = Titleholders (1937–1972), WES = Western Open (1937–1967)

PGA TOUR CAREER EARNINGS*

1. Tiger Woods — $112,205,724
2. Phil Mickelson — $87,617,019
3. Vijay Singh — $70,952,528
4. Jim Furyk — $68,098,747
5. Dustin Johnson — $53,363,689
6. Ernie Els — $49,016,137
7. Sergio Garcia — $47,974,884
8. Adam Scott — $47,913,678
9. Justin Rose — $46,699,435
10. Davis Love III — $44,637,954

LPGA TOUR CAREER EARNINGS*

1. Annika Sorenstam — $22,573,192
2. Karrie Webb — $20,217,402
3. Cristie Kerr — $19,484,929
4. Lorena Ochoa — $14,863,331
5. Suzann Pettersen — $14,831,968

*Through July 2018

JUSTIN ROSE

A second-place finish at the 2018 British Open (he actually tied with two others at 6 under par) signalled that Rose is not finished adding to his growing career money total. The English golfer won two other events in 2018 to bring his career total to nine PGA victories. The pair of wins also matched his best single-season total. He has also finished in the top three of 33 other tournaments. That sort of consistent excellent play moved him up to No. 5 in the world golf rankings. It also moved him onto the list of the top 10 money-winners for the first time.

TENNIS

WINNING NEVER GETS OLD . . .

. . . and neither, it seems, does Roger Federer. The great Swiss star beat Marian Čilić at the Australian Open. It was Federer's 20th Grand Slam, but he still got emotional at the trophy ceremony. "The fairy tale continues for my family and me," he said as he wiped away tears.

2018 Men's Tennis

It was old home time at the men's Grand Slam events in 2018. The three players who have mostly dominated tennis for the past decade continued to thrill fans and amaze opponents. **Roger Federer**, **Rafael Nadal**, and **Novak Djokovic** have had a nearly complete hold on the Grand Slams for years. Few sports have seen a group of athletes be this good together for so long. The trend continued in 2018.

At 36, Federer seemed like he was finally coming back to earth. The other two stars were trading the Grand Slams back and forth. Then he won two in 2017 and began 2018 by winning the Australian Open. The title extended his all-time record of 20 Grand Slam singles titles. The Swiss star had to work hard for his sixth title Down Under. He did not lose a set until **Marin Čilić** pushed him to five sets in the final.

Nadal is from Spain, but clearly feels right at home in France. He won his 11th French Open in June. That's way more than any other player. It was also his 17th Grand Slam title, trailing only Federer.

With the first two stars already winners, it was up to Djokovic at Wimbledon to earn his own 2018 Grand Slam. He had been upset by an 83rd-seeded player in

Anderson was wiped out, but he won.

France, so he was eager to prove he was still among the best. He proved it big-time. Djokovic cruised through the early rounds and then beat **Kevin Anderson** in straight sets in the final. His 13th career Grand Slam puts him one behind his boyhood idol, **Pete Sampras**.

You might forgive Anderson for being tired. The tall South African won the semifinal over **John Isner** in the second-longest match in Wimbledon history. The two battled for more than six-and-a-half hours! The final tie-breaking game took 50 points to decide! Both men were exhausted afterward, but it was still Anderson's best finish at a major. Might he be the one to topple the big three someday?

2018 MEN'S GRAND SLAMS

AUSTRALIAN OPEN	**Roger Federer**
FRENCH OPEN	**Rafael Nadal**
WIMBLEDON	**Novak Djokovic**
US OPEN	**Novak Djokovic**

2018 Women's Tennis

Wozniacki broke through for her first Slam title.

The most famous woman in tennis in 2018 was **Alexis Ohanian Jr**. Never heard of her? That's okay, she's not much more than a year old. Her mom, though, is pretty famous: **Serena Williams**. Williams gave birth to Alexis in September 2017. Williams later had several surgeries following the birth. All that kept her from returning to the court for more than six months. Opponents took advantage of the top player in the world being absent.

Caroline Wozniacki won her first Grand Slam by capturing the Australian Open. She was also the first player from Denmark, man or woman, to capture a Grand Slam tennis singles title. She beat **Simona Halep** of Romania, who later went on to win the 2018 French Open. There, Halep beat rising American player **Sloane Stephens**.

In July at Wimbledon, Williams was back! She made it all the way to the final, where she was upset by **Angelique Kerber**. She continued to get stronger, though, so the "Alexis Holiday" was soon over for women's tennis.

2018 WOMEN'S GRAND SLAMS

AUSTRALIAN OPEN	**Caroline Wozniacki**
FRENCH OPEN	**Simona Halep**
WIMBLEDON	**Angelique Kerber**
US OPEN	**Naomi Osaka**

Kerber (right) stunned Williams at Wimbledon.

Tennis Notes

FEDERATION CUP

The US women had made the finals of the Federation Cup three times since winning the tournament in 2000. The Fed Cup puts nation against nation in a team tennis event. The Americans had won more Cups than any other country, but they were in a 17-year drought. The 2017 team determined to change that.

The US advanced to the final match against Belarus by defeating Germany and the Czech Republic. The big star was **Coco Vandeweghe**. She won all of her singles matches throughout the early rounds.

Against Belarus in the final, Vandeweghe beat **Aryna Sabalenka** and **Aliaksandra Sasnovich** in singles. Then, with the title on the line, Vandeweghe teamed with **Shelby Rogers** to defeat the Belarus doubles team for the deciding points. The US was back on top again!

RISING STARS

In both men's and women's tennis, a few stars have been hogging all the trophies lately. Who's coming up to challenge them? Here are a few young players to watch.

Is Germany's Zverev the next big thing in tennis?

→ Germany's **Alexander Zverev** is only 21, but reached No. 3 in the world in 2018. He had won eight tournaments through mid-2018, but was still seeking his first major.

→ Croatia's **Borna Coric** has been rising steadily, too, reaching his highest ranking in July 2018.

→ **Jelena Ostapenko** of Latvia reached the 2018 Wimbledon semifinals and a No. 5 ranking. And she's only 19!

→ American **Sloane Stephens** cracked into the top five in 2018 and she figures to stay there. Her 2017 US Open win makes her a star to watch for sure.

Grand Slams

ALL-TIME GRAND SLAM CHAMPIONSHIPS (MEN)

	AUSTRALIAN	FRENCH	WIMBLEDON	US OPEN	TOTAL
Roger **FEDERER**	6	1	8	5	**20**
Rafael **NADAL**	1	11	2	2	**16**
Pete **SAMPRAS**	2	0	7	5	**14**
Novak **DJOKOVIC**	6	1	4	3	**14**
Roy **EMERSON**	6	2	2	2	**12**
Björn **BORG**	0	6	5	0	**11**
Rod **LAVER**	3	2	4	2	**11**
Bill **TILDEN**	0	0	3	7	**10**
Andre **AGASSI**	4	1	1	2	**8**
Jimmy **CONNORS**	1	0	2	5	**8**
Ivan **LENDL**	2	3	0	3	**8**
Fred **PERRY**	1	1	3	3	**8**
Ken **ROSEWALL**	4	2	0	2	**8**

ROD LAVER If winning all four Grand Slams in a single year is the measure of tennis greatness, then this Australian lefty is the best player ever! Laver is the only person to accomplish the feat twice. In 1962, he did it while playing as an amateur. In 1969, he matched that as a pro. He was No. 1 in the world from 1964 to 1970. How good was he? Since the Grand Slams were amateurs only until 1968, he was not allowed to play in them from 1963-68! Imagine how many he might have won!

ALL-TIME GRAND SLAM CHAMPIONSHIPS (WOMEN)

	AUSTRALIAN	FRENCH	WIMBLEDON	US OPEN	TOTAL
Margaret Smith **COURT**	11	5	3	5	24
Serena **WILLIAMS**	7	3	7	6	23
Steffi **GRAF**	4	6	7	5	22
Helen Wills **MOODY**	0	4	8	7	19
Chris **EVERT**	2	7	3	6	18
Martina **NAVRATILOVA**	3	2	9	4	18
Billie Jean **KING**	1	1	6	4	12
Maureen **CONNOLLY**	1	2	3	3	9
Monica **SELES**	4	3	0	2	9
Suzanne **LENGLEN**	0	2*	6	0	8
Molla Bjurstedt **MALLORY**	0	0	0	8	8

*Also won four French titles before 1925; in those years, the tournament was open only to French nationals.

Billie Jean King

Billie Jean King's tennis career was Hall of Fame stuff for sure. She won 39 Grand Slam titles in singles, doubles, and mixed doubles. Her first came in Wimbledon in 1966, when she reached the No. 1 ranking. She added 11 more Grand Slam singles wins and took part in numerous Federation Cups. She was the first female tennis player to be the Sports Illustrated Athlete of the Year. However, her biggest impact might have been off the court. King was one of the founders of the women's pro tour and a leader in the fight for equal rights. In 2009, she received the Presidential Medal of Freedom for her hard work.

SUDDEN STARS

OZZIE ALBIES
BRAVES

A young Atlanta Braves team made a lot of noise in the summer of 2018. One of the biggest noisemakers was this second-year pro. Albies was only 21 in mid-2018, but he made his first All-Star team. At the break, he led the NL in runs and doubles, while hitting .280. Albies is one of the few MLB players to come from the Caribbean island of Curaçao.

MATHEW BARZAL
ISLANDERS

The last time an NHL rookie had three five-point games there was no such thing as TV, let alone the Internet! No first-year player had done that since 1919, but Barzal did. His hot scoring power helped him win the Calder Trophy as the league's top rookie. He led all rookies in goals and assists and could have had more if not for a back injury in March. Still, his 63 assists were tied for second-most all-time by a first-year player.

TIERNA DAVIDSON
US SOCCER

Talk about having a good year! Davidson led her Stanford team to the NCAA championship in the fall of 2017. She was named the tournament's top defender. She helped the US Under-20 team qualify for the U-20 World Cup. Then she was called up to the senior national team . . . and she was still only 19! In early 2018, she helped the US win the SheBelieves Cup, making a huge save off the line in the clinching game. The Women's World Cup is in France in 2019; watch for this young star to make an impact.

ALVIN KAMARA
SAINTS RB

When Kamara was drafted in the third round by the Saints, fans figured he would sit a lot. The team had two top running backs. He had other plans. Once Kamara got on the field, he made the most of his chances. He scored 14 total touchdowns and averaged a league-best 6.1 yards per carry. He also brought home honors for top offensive rookie and a spot in the Pro Bowl.

SUNG HYUN PARK
LPGA

Talk about a hot start! Park was in her first year on the LPGA Tour when she won the 2017 US Women's Open! By November, she was the top-ranked golfer in the world. She had been a star in her native Korea, but showed she more than belonged on the big stage. Park was the first LPGA player since Nancy Lopez way back in 1978 to be Rookie AND Player of the Year. She added another major at the 2018 Women's PGA Championship.

BEN SIMMONS

76ERS

Good things are worth waiting for. In 2016, the 76ers took Simmons No. 1 in the NBA Draft. Then he hurt his foot before their first game and missed a whole season. When he finally got on the court, he really stood out. The forward's all-around skills at both ends of the court led Philly back to the playoffs for the first time since 2012.

JUAN SOTO
NATIONALS

Ozzie Albies (page 168) is one young MLB star; here's another! Soto was only 19 when he was called up to the Nats in May. He was in the Double-A minors at the time, but he quickly proved he belonged. In his second career at-bat, he hit his first big-league homer! Opponents saw how good he was. He was the first teenager to be walked on purpose since 2007! Watch for big things in DC from Soto!

A'JA Wilson
LAS VEGAS ACES

Moving from college basketball to the pros can be tough for young players. Not so much for Wilson. After becoming the best player in University of South Carolina history, she was the No. 1 overall pick of the WNBA Draft by the Aces. Wilson found the pro game a bit faster, but she adjusted quickly. By midseason, she was in the top five in the league in scoring. What will she do when she really gets settled in? Watch out,

MUDDY IN MAY!
In a driving rainstorm, Justify slopped home to win the Kentucky Derby. That was just the start of a magical streak of success for the three-year-old horse. Under jockey Mike Smith, Justify went on to become only the second horse to win the famous Triple Crown after American Pharoah ended a 37-year drought in 2015.

OTHER SPORTS

Justify (on the right) flashed past the competition in the Belmont Stakes.

Horse Racing

It happened again! The biggest prize in horse racing was not claimed for 37 years. Then **American Pharoah** won the Triple Crown in 2014. Would racing fans have to wait another 37 years?

Nope!

With a thundering win in the Belmont Stakes, **Justify** won the 13th Triple Crown in history. The big win in New York followed first-place finishes in the Kentucky Derby and the Preakness. Up to that point, Justify had never lost a race, making him the second undefeated Triple Crown champ.

Jockey **Mike Smith** rode Justify to all three wins. At 52, he became the oldest jockey to win racing's biggest prize. The pair won the Derby by 2.5 lengths and squeaked ahead by a half-length in the Preakness. More than 20 horses have won those two races only to fall in the longer and harder Belmont. But Justify was up to the challenge and won easily.

The link between Justify and Pharoah was trainer **Bob Baffert**. The veteran guided the Triple Crown winner in 2014 and repeated the feat in 2018. Baffert became only the second trainer with a pair of Triple Crowns.

Rugby Sevens World Cup

Rugby is one of the world's most popular sports, but it's still trying to catch on in the United States. American fans—and lots of overseas visitors—got a chance to see the best in the world in action in San Francisco. The Rugby World Sevens championship was held there in July 2018. The top 24 nations sent their teams to the Bay Area to battle for the big prize.

Rugby is more often played with 15 players on a side, with lots of scrums and lower scores. Rugby sevens is played with, that's right, seven players. That leaves lots of room to run and the games often feature exciting long-distance sprints for "tries" (that's what they call scores in rugby).

The men's tournament ended with a familiar champion on top: New Zealand. The other country "down under" has won titles in sevens before, along with the full-size Rugby World Cup. The sport is huge in the island

All Blacks action from the men's final.

The Black Ferns ran away with the title.

nation. Its teams are called the All Blacks after the color of their jerseys. In the final, New Zealand beat England 33–12.

The US men's team did better than expected, reaching the quarterfinals. England beat the Americans 24–19, but needed overtime to do it.

The women's championship trophy will be on the same airplane home. New Zealand's Black Ferns swamped France 29–0 in the final. The US women's team made it to the semifinals.

Esports

"Stadium" Fortnite?

Fortnite: Battle Royale became the hottest game of 2018 as millions jumped in to play the video game. The competition moved out of the living room onto a much bigger stage at a pro-am event in Los Angeles. Stars from the NFL and NBA joined other celebrities in playing the game in front of a huge crowd at a stadium that's usually home to soccer. More than 1.7 million fans watched online. Famed gamer Ninja (left) won the event, which raised more than $1 million for charity.

One for the Home Folks

At CounterStrike Boston, Cloud9 became the first team from North America to win a major event. In front of a packed house of cheering local fans, they beat FaZe Clan in a dramatic three-game series. Cloud9 came in as a big underdog, but beat four of the top teams in the world to carry home the trophy.

LONGEST GAME EVER!

SKT is a legend in League of Legends. They've been at or near the top of dozens of big events, including the Worlds. So it was no surprise that they were part of a record-setting event in South Korea in January 2018. The third game of their series against Jin Air lasted more than 90 minutes, the longest game ever in competition.

Lacrosse

World Championships

The World Championship of this action-packed sport has been tossed back and forth like a lacrosse ball since 2002. The US and Canada each had two titles in that time frame, in alternate tournaments. In 2018, the two powerhouses kept the pattern going. With just one second left in the championship game, **Tom Schreiber** of the US scored to give the Americans the title. Team USA's **Michael Erhardt** was named the tournament MVP.

NLL IS A RUSH!

There's a new dynasty in sports! And no, we're not talking about the Golden State Warriors. For the third time in the past four seasons, the Saskatchewan Rush won the National Lacrosse (NLL) title. They knocked off the Rochester Knighthawks in the championship series.

It's been a great run for the Rush. They won in 2015 when they were in Edmonton. After their move to a new city, they kept winning, taking home the 2016 title. Last year, they lost in the finals, but in 2018 jumped back on top. **Mark Matthews** had eight assists in the deciding game. MVP **Jeff Shattler** had eight goals in the final series.

BMX

WORLD CHAMPIONSHIPS

The world's best BMX riders gathered in an unlikely place to see who would be the fastest on the track. The 2018 World Championships were held in Baku in the country of Azerbaijan (look it up on a map!). Two countries proved to be the big winners: France's **Sylvain André** won the top men's event, while **Leo Garoyan** was the junior men's winner. Two riders from the Netherlands, **Laura Smulders** and **Indy Scheepers**, won the women's top and junior levels, respectively. Now that their sport is in the Olympics, riders like these hope to add gold to their trophy cases in 2020.

USA BMX

At the end of the 2017 season, a stack of great riders hoisted their trophies in America's national racing circuit.

Pro: Connor Fields became the first American in nine years to earn the top spot. Raised in Las Vegas, he has been moving up the ranks steadily.

Women Pro: Alise Post won her first national championship with a steady series of high finishes.

Vet Pro: BMX is not just for the young riders. In this category, riders have to be over 33 years old to qualify. **Cristian Becerine** learned the sport in his native Argentina, and became a top international rider. His 2017 championship was the fifth of his great career and his third in a row.

Connor Fields jumped to the top of the Pro ranks in 2017.

Bass Fishing

This is a sport? Well, it's a pretty intense competition that calls for stamina, hand-eye coordination, and strength. Sounds pretty sporty! The biggest and most popular fishing contests go after hard-fighting bass fish. B.A.S.S., the group that runs the tournaments, is celebrating its 50th year in 2019!

The biggest B.A.S.S. event is the Bassmaster Classic, the "Super Bowl" of fishing, as some say. In the 2017 event, **Jordan Lee** pulled off one of the greatest comebacks ever. In these events, anglers have a time limit to pull in as many fish as they can. Most weight wins. For a while, Lee was more than 13 pounds back, but reeled in enough to

World Record for a Kid!

Maverick Yoakum not only has an awesome name, he is also an awesome angler. In April 2018, while fishing with his dad, Maverick landed a fish that was 10 pounds, three ounces. It was a river redhorse out of the Tavern Creek in Missouri. When they got back to the dock, the pair looked it up and found that it might be a world record! The International Game Fish Association will decide, but it looked pretty good. Nice going, Mav!

Jordan Lee caught a big trophy along with a lot of fish!

win the final weigh-off. Then in 2018, he repeated the feat! He was in sixth place, but pulled five bass in quick order. That gave him a winning total of more than 47 pounds!

Lee is only the third person ever to win the event twice.

NCAA Highlights: Men

We've already covered football and basketball, but there are lots of other scholar-athletes who don't always grab the headlines! The NCAA hosts top-level college championships in two dozen sports. Here are a few of the highlights from the Division I competition in the 2017–18 school year.

Moldauer dominated the finals for OU.

their fourth national championship in a row in 2018. Their overall winning streak reached an amazing 97 straight meets. South Korean **Yul Moldauer** won four individual events to key Oklahoma's record-tying twelfth title in all.

ICE HOCKEY: Minnesota Duluth

With the Frozen Four held in nearby St. Paul, Minnesota Duluth thrilled the home-state fans. The Bulldogs scored the first two goals in the championship game, then held off Notre Dame 2–1 behind some superb goaltending by **Hunter Shepard**. It was Minnesota Duluth's second national title.

GOLF: Oklahoma State

Oklahoma State has a proud golf history. Cowboys alumni include PGA stars **Rickie Fowler**, **Charles Howell III**, and **Peter Uihlein**. Don't be surprised if the school soon adds more names to that list after winning its eleventh team championship in 2018. The Cowboys swept Alabama 5–0 in the title match.

GYMNASTICS: Oklahoma

For four years, Oklahoma has been unbeatable—literally! The Sooners won

Other National Champions

BASEBALL: **Oregon State**
CROSS COUNTRY: **Northern Arizona**
FENCING (MEN & WOMEN): **Notre Dame**
LACROSSE: **Yale**
RIFLE (MEN & WOMEN): **Kentucky**
SKIING (MEN & WOMEN): **Denver**
TENNIS: **Wake Forest**
TRACK AND FIELD (INDOOR): **Florida**
TRACK AND FIELD (OUTDOOR): **Georgia**
VOLLEYBALL: **Long Beach State**
WATER POLO: **UCLA**

Here's hoping Texas coach Eddie Reese was wearing a waterproof watch!

SOCCER: Stanford

This one was a long time coming, but for the Cardinal, it was worth the wait. Stanford battled Indiana through two halves and one full overtime of scoreless play. Finally, in the 103rd minute, the Cardinal's **Sam Werner** flipped a shot over the head of the Hoosiers' keeper and just under the crossbar. And the celebration began! One week earlier, the Cardinal women's team also won the NCAA title. Stanford became the first school to take both soccer championships in the same year.

SWIMMING & DIVING: Texas

Everybody into the pool! That's how Texas celebrated after winning the national title . . . for the fourth year in a row. Freshman **Austin Katz** helped rally the Longhorns past California by winning the 200-meter backstroke on the final night of competition. After Texas won its 14th title in **Eddie Reese**'s 40 years as coach, it was time for a celebratory splash. The entire team leapt into the pool—and sang the school fight song!

◀ WRESTLING: Penn State

Penn State has built a dynasty. When **Bo Nickal** pinned Ohio State's **Myles Martin** (left) in the final of the 184-pound class, the Nittany Lions were national champs again. It was their seventh title in the last eight years.

NCAA Highlights: Women

BOWLING: Vanderbilt

The Commodores won with the help of a clutch effort by sophomore **Maria Bulanova**. Vanderbilt was facing elimination against McKendree University in Game 6 of the best-of-seven final. That's when Bulanova approached the line in the tenth frame. She rolled one strike, and then another, and the Commodores squeezed out a win to force a decisive seventh game. They won that one easily to claim the championship.

CROSS COUNTRY: New Mexico

Ednah Kurgat capped a perfect season—she won all five races she entered—and helped New Mexico win the team title. Kurgat set a new NCAA Division I championship record with a time of 19:19.5 in the 6K race. That was eight seconds faster than the previous record! Bad news for Lobos' opponents: The native of Kenya still has two years of eligibility remaining.

GOLF: Arizona

There might be nothing better in sports than a walk-off victory to win a championship. Arizona and Alabama were tied 2–2 in the championship match when the decisive fifth pairing went into extra holes. **Haley Moore** sank the winning putt to give the Wildcats the title. It was the first for **Laura Ianello** as Arizona's head coach. But she knew the feeling: She was a player on the school's title-winning team in 2000.

◀ GYMNASTICS: UCLA

For the Bruins, this outcome was, well . . . perfect! UCLA needed senior **Christine Peng-Peng Lee** to score at least 9.975—out of a possible 10—on the final routine of the night, the balance beam. Lee was flawless, posting a championship-winning 10, to keep Oklahoma from winning a third consecutive title.

Other National Champions

BEACH VOLLEYBALL: **UCLA**
FIELD HOCKEY: **Connecticut**
ICE HOCKEY: **Clarkson**
LACROSSE: **James Madison**
SOCCER: **Stanford**
SOFTBALL: **Florida State**
SWIMMING & DIVING: **Stanford**
TENNIS: **Stanford**
TRACK AND FIELD (INDOOR): **Georgia**
VOLLEYBALL: **Nebraska**
WATER POLO: **USC**

ROWING: California

A show of sportsmanship was the big story at this championship. Upon arriving one morning for competition, the Yale team discovered that its Varsity Eight boat had been damaged by a storm. There were four holes in the boat! Rowers and coaches from

several other squads, including the eventual-champion Golden Bears, teamed up to help get the Yale crew back on the water. California's title was its second in three years.

◀ TRACK AND FIELD (OUTDOOR): USC

What a finish! The Trojans entered the final event of the meet, the 4 x 400-meter relay, needing a victory to win the title. One hundred yards from the tape, it seemed hopeless— the Trojans were more than 30 yards behind. But that's when anchor runner **Kendall Ellis** (left) shifted into high gear. Her incredible finishing kick edged the Purdue team by seven-hundredths of a second. It gave USC the national championship by the narrowest of margins: one point over runner-up Georgia and two points over third-place Stanford.

Kurgat (center) was the key to the Lobos' cross-country win.

Big Events 2018-19

September 2018

6 Pro Football
NFL regular season begins
with Atlanta at defending-
champion Philadelphia

8-9 Tennis
US Open finals,
New York, New York

9-16 Rowing
World Championships,
Plovdiv, Bulgaria

23-30 Cycling
Road World Cycling
Championships, Innsbruck,
Austria

27-30 Golf
Ryder Cup, Saint-Quentin-en-
Yvelines, France

TBA Basketball
WNBA Finals,
Teams and sites TBA

October 2018

2 Baseball
MLB postseason begins
(Wild Card playoff games,
League Division Series,
League Championship Series,
World Series)

3 Ice Hockey
NHL regular season begins

13 Swim/Bike/Run
Ironman Triathlon World
Championship, Kailua-Kona,
Hawaii

25– Gymnastics
Nov. 3 World Artistic Gymnastics
Championships, Doha, Qatar

TBA Basketball
NBA regular season begins

TBA Ice Hockey
NWHL regular season begins

November 2018

4 Running
New York City Marathon

11-18 Tennis
ATP World Tour Finals,
London, England

18 Stock Car Racing
Ford Ecoboost 400,
final race of 2018 NASCAR
Chase for the Cup,
Homestead, Florida

25 Auto Racing
Abu Dhabi Grand Prix,
final race of Formula 1 season

25 Football
Grey Cup, CFL Championship
Game, Edmonton, Alberta,
Canada

30 College Football
Pac-12 Championship Game,
Santa Clara, California

30, College Soccer
Dec. 2 Women's College Cup,
Orlando, Florida

December 2018

1 College Football

ACC Championship Game,
Charlotte, NC

Big 12 Championship Game,
Arlington, Texas

Big Ten Championship Game,
Indianapolis, Indiana

SEC Championship Game,
Atlanta, Georgia

6–15 Rodeo
National Finals Rodeo,
Las Vegas, Nevada

7, 9 College Soccer
Men's College Cup,
Santa Barbara, California

8 Soccer
MLS Cup, teams and site TBA

29 College Football
College Football Playoff
Semifinal; Cotton Bowl,
Arlington, Texas

College Football Playoff
Semifinal; Orange Bowl,
Miami, Florida

Peach Bowl, Atlanta, Georgia

January 2019

1 College Football

Fiesta Bowl, Glendale, Arizona

Rose Bowl, Pasadena, California

Sugar Bowl, New Orleans,
Louisiana

5–6 Pro Football
NFL Wild Card Playoff
Weekend

7 College Football
College Football Playoff
Championship Game,
Santa Clara, California

12–13 Pro Football
NFL Divisional Playoff Weekend

18–27 Figure Skating
US Figure Skating
Championships,
Detroit, Michigan

20 Pro Football
NFL Conference
Championship Games

24–27 Action Sports
Winter X Games,
Aspen, Colorado

26 Hockey
NHL All-Star Game,
San Jose, California

26–27 Tennis
Australian Open finals

27 Pro Football
NFL Pro Bowl, Orlando, Florida

TBA Baseball
Caribbean Series, Venezuela

February 2019

3 Pro Football
Super Bowl LIII,
Atlanta, Georgia

5–17 Skiing
Apline World Ski
Championships, Åre, Sweden

17 Basketball
NBA All-Star Game,
Charlotte, North Carolina

17 Stock Car Racing
(NASCAR) Daytona 500,
Daytona Beach, Florida

March 2019

18–24 Figure Skating
World Figure Skating
Championships, Saitama, Japan

20–21 Baseball
Major League Baseball's
regular season schedule begins
with two games in Japan
between Oakland and Seattle,
Tokyo, Japan

31 Baseball
Major League Baseball,
Opening Day

April 2019

5, 7 College Basketball
NCAA Women's Final Four,
Tampa, Florida

6, 8 College Basketball
NCAA Men's Final Four,
San Antonio, Texas

11–14 Golf
The Masters, Augusta, Georgia

TBA Ice Hockey
NHL playoffs begin

May 2019

3–19 Ice Hockey
IIHF World Championships,
Slovakia

4 Horse Racing
Kentucky Derby, Churchill
Downs, Louisville, Kentucky

16–19 Golf
PGA Championship,
Farmingdale, New York

18 Horse Racing
Preakness Stakes,
Pimlico Race Course,
Baltimore, Maryland

26 IndyCar Racing
Indianapolis 500,
Indianapolis, Indiana

27– Golf
June 2 US Women's Open,
Charleston, South Carolina

June 2019

1 Soccer
UEFA Champions League Final,
Madrid, Spain

7– **Soccer**
July 7 Women's World Cup,
France

8 Horse Racing
Belmont Stakes,
Belmont Park,
Elmont, New York

8–9 Tennis
French Open Finals,
Paris, France

13–16 Golf
US Open Championship,
Pebble Beach, California

14 College Baseball
College World Series begins,
Omaha, Nebraska

20–23 Golf
Women's PGA Championship,
Chaska, Minnesota

29 Cycling
Tour de France begins,
Brussels

TBA Basketball
NBA Finals, sites TBA

July 2019

9 Baseball
MLB All-Star Game,
Cleveland, Ohio

13–14 Tennis
Wimbledon Championships
finals, London, England

18–21 Golf
British Open Championship,
Portrush, Northern Ireland

TBA Action Sports
Summer X Games,
Minneapolis, Minnesota

August 2019

TBA Baseball
Little League World Series,
Williamsport, Pennsylvania

Note: Dates and sites subject to change. TBA: To be announced. Actual dates of event not available at press time.

Produced by Shoreline Publishing Group LLC

Santa Barbara, California

www.shorelinepublishing.com

President/Editorial Director: James Buckley, Jr.

Designed by Tom Carling, www.carlingdesign.com

The *Scholastic Year in Sports* text was written by

James Buckley, Jr.

Editorial assistance and text for Action Sports and Calendar: **Jim Gigliotti**.

Fact-checking: **Matt Marini**. Thanks to **Beth Adelman**, **Zachary Vanderberg**,

and **Craig Zeichner** for their help with the NHL chapter.

Thanks to team captain Amanda Shih, Jael Fogle, Deborah Kurosz, Emily Teresa, Stephen Chin, and the superstars at Scholastic for all their championship work! Photo research was done by the author.

Photography Credits